This is one of the most helpful, biblical, and insightful books I have read on the subject of what to do in the midst of crisis and trials. For everyone who experiences the onslaught of "giant despair" and the "slough of despond" (Bunyan), this book offers hope, encouragement, and practical guidance.

Bruce W. Gay, Ph.D.
Assistant Professor of Criminology and Criminal Justice
University of Texas at Arlington

Read this book now, even if you're not presently hurting, because it will help prepare you to keep believing when the tough times come—and they will. This book helped me to realize that many of my "why" questions are never meant to be answered. The real question becomes, "Am I going to keep believing even though I don't understand?"

Brian Bill
Church Planter, Project Aztec, Mexico City

Keep Believing is a book for those trying to continue to believe or perhaps to find God in the midst of evil, struggles, and pain. Pastoral, personal, and practical, you will find encouragement here.

Dr. Michael P. Green
Associate Professor, Practical Theology
Trinity Evangelical Divinity School

With this book, Ray Pritchard offers a helping hand for all who struggle with grief, fear, or loss. Keep Believing makes it perfectly clear that although we sometimes cannot understand the will of God, He will never forsake those who are faithful. It helps us to understand the mystery of undeserved suffering and strengthens us to never lose faith in Him, even in our darkest hour.

Ulrike G. McNamara, Ph.D., Research Associate
Barry P. McNamara, Ph.D., Research Associate
University of Maryland at Baltimore

Keep Believing is written for all of us who struggle with "the stuff" that life is made of.
- For those who question, there are biblical answers.
- For those who doubt, there is assurance.
- For those who get discouraged, there is encouragement.
- And for those who lose focus, there is direction.

Tom Phillips, Director
Word of Life Fellowship, Hudson, Florida

D1005335

Ray Pritchard's insightful writing is a life preserver thrown out to all of us who are drowning in the everyday struggles of life. I have struggled and I have doubted God at times. But this book has renewed my faith in God's promise to be with me come what may.

E. Howard Harvey
Senior Vice President, Creative Group, Inc.

Dr. Pritchard demonstrates his uncommon ability to integrate his Bible knowledge and communication skills, and his own experiences and those of his pastoral family in a book that speaks to the heart. Keep Believing *is for anyone who has ever, is currently, or will ever go through the extreme challenges of life. Dr. Pritchard points the reader to the fact that God always has our best interests at heart, no matter how bad the circumstances seem.*

Bettye Megason
Computer Consultant, Dallas, Texas

Pain, illness, and trouble come to all of us in different sizes and shapes. This book is a wonderful resource to help everyone going through difficult times find God's grace instead of allowing their faith in God to be sidetracked. Pastor Ray enables us to keep on keeping on when the roadblocks block our view of our heavenly Father's presence.

Dr. Richard A. Todd
Minister of Parish Life
St. Andrew's Presbyterian Church
Newport Beach, California

In Keep Believing, *Dr. Pritchard presents men and women of faith and their questions and struggles. These are juxtaposed with scriptural principles that shed light and understanding on God, who "causes all things to work together for good."* Keep Believing *will provide insight to help you strengthen your faith when life is rough.*

Dr. Tom Renard
Pediatric Surgeon, Dallas, Texas

This insightful work, borne from experience, expertly encourages Christians toward faith first *in our search for peace amid life's inevitable struggles. In* Keep Believing, *my longtime friend Ray Pritchard shares beautifully and creatively scriptural solutions to life's struggles. His qualifications are validated by his experiences. This is an inspiring and fresh look at the awesome truth of God's Sovereignty!*

Rev. Ron Lambe
Associate Pastor
Istrouma Baptist Church, Baton Rouge, Louisiana

RAY PRITCHARD

MOODY PRESS

CHICAGO

In honor of my mother

and in memory of my father

from a very grateful son

Dr. Ray Pritchard (D.Min., Talbot School of Theology; graduate of Tennessee Temple University and Dallas Theological Seminary) is senior pastor of Calvary Memorial Church, Oak Park, Illinois. His span of experience—from ministering overseas, to guest-lecturing, to appearing on talk shows—provides a unique supply of knowledge and insight. Pritchard is author of *The Road Best Traveled*, *Names of the Holy Spirit*, and *Man of Honor*. He and his wife, Marlene, have three sons: Joshua, Mark, and Nicholas.

CONTENTS

FOREWORD

I have been waiting for someone to write this book! And I already have a list of people who need its message *now!*

Every writer has a target audience in mind, defined either by age, class, or specific need. This book encompasses virtually everyone. Those who are facing tragedies will find it comforting; those whose lives are momentarily free from tears will be better prepared to help others who are struggling with the harsh realities of life.

Pastor Pritchard takes the promises of God in one hand and the anguishing questions of life in the other and brings them together, convinced that the Bible has something to say to us when life tumbles in. You will get the feeling that you are eavesdropping, listening in as he pours salve on fresh wounds of sorrow, comforting those who find their faith sliding on the slope of a question mark.

What makes this book special is its compelling realism. Every reader will be persuaded that Pastor Pritchard has indeed heard all of us. He has sat with us in a hospital waiting room, hearing the news that a child has died; he has listened to a man grieve over the death of his marriage. He knows the keen disappointment of unanswered prayer. He knows that we cannot comfort others by trying to minimize the pain of loneliness and personal anguish. He does not preach at us but takes us by the hand and leads us back to where we need to be.

This book has added credibility because the author does not pretend to have all the answers. Rather, he points us to God and reminds us that we have nowhere else to go. With God there are few answers; without God there are none. So in the presence of the Almighty, we do not have all of our questions answered, but we do find help and comfort. On our knees we will come to agree with the man who said, "As Christians we live by promises, not explanations."

Finally, readers will appreciate Pastor Pritchard's writing style. He not only communicates information but paints pictures, so that we can identify with the issues discussed. I found myself saying, "Yes . . . I've felt that way . . . and those are the questions that have often plagued my mind."

Read it! Study it! Share it!

Dr. ERWIN W. LUTZER
SENIOR PASTOR
THE MOODY CHURCH

ACKNOWLEDGMENTS

I have received enormous encouragement from Lisa King in the preparation of this book. I owe her more than she knows. Special thanks also to Greg Thornton, Jim Bell, Suzanne Dowd, Evie Knottnerus, Julie Ieron, and Anne Scherich of Moody Press for many acts of kindness. My dear friend Brian Bill gave wise counsel at several points. Because this book was written during some trying times in my own life, I am grateful to my wife and my three sons for their loving support, and to the elders of Calvary Memorial Church for allowing me the time to finish this project.

INTRODUCTION

Everyone has a story to tell, even the people who seem to smile all the time. This is one of the first things a young pastor learns when he graduates from seminary and begins his ministry. Some people look so well-adjusted and happy that you think they don't have a care in the world. But they do. If you work with people long enough, you discover that even the "perfect" people know all about sorrow and heartache.

If you stay in one church long enough, you begin to hear the stories. Everybody has one. A tale of sadness or of failure. A story of a broken marriage, of a child with an incurable disease, of alcohol abuse, of crushing financial disaster, of loved ones far from God, of dreams dashed on the jagged rocks of reality. Every face has its own secret story. The pastor soon learns to look behind the smile for the shadows that are always there. Sometimes it takes a while, and sometimes he hears about it second- or thirdhand, but over time, the truth comes out and the story is told. But the pastor is not surprised, for behind his own smiling face are many stories, some so painful they are never told, others only alluded to here and there, little whispers of past difficulties that the discerning listener hears even if he doesn't fully understand.

This book is addressed to those people who want to know what God has to say about their pain, their sadness, their failures, and their unanswered prayers. Many of them have secretly given up on God because they feel He has wounded them and can no longer be trusted. Others grimly hold on to faith because they have nowhere else to turn.

To all those people, God says, "I am still here and I care about you." The chapters of this book reinforce that truth by bringing the reader face-to-face with God. Some of the chapters sketch out the problems of life, some tackle difficult theological issues, and still others revisit well-known biblical texts that call us to a higher view of God and a deep trust in our Creator. One chapter was born on a hot summer afternoon in southern California during a doctoral seminar when Vernon Grounds gave the first explanation of Romans 8:28 that actually made sense to me. The final chapter was written some years ago in response to a pulpit committee that wanted my statement of faith. As I sat down to write it—during Easter week—I could not stop thinking about a dear friend who was dying of cancer. The result is my answer to the question, "Pastor Ray, how can you still believe in God?"

After nineteen years as a pastor, after speaking around the country and talking with hundreds of people about their problems, I have come to the conviction that the biggest barrier to faith is life itself. More than once I have been asked "Why?" only to shake my head in wonderment at the strange acts of God. I cannot explain why Len Hoppe died from cancer at the age of forty-two, leaving behind a wife and four children. But Len died as a Christian, still believing in God to the very end. I have seen that happen often enough to know that the Christian faith provides answers that cannot be found anywhere else.

If I possess any special qualification for writing this book, it is that I have spent hours pondering these questions with friends who cling to faith as their last resort. Needless to say, these chapters are not the last word on the subject of suffering and the Christian faith. They represent the things I have learned by spending time with the people of God in some very difficult moments. When you have finished this book, you will still have many questions, but I hope you will be encouraged to keep on believing in God.

1

WHEN LIFE TUMBLES IN, WHAT THEN?

When his wife died, he didn't know at first how he would survive. Although he was a minister and had helped many others through times of crisis, now he faced his own personal moment of truth. How would he reconcile his own loss with the Christian faith he claimed to believe? What would he say to his own grieving congregation?

The year was 1927. The place, Aberdeen, Scotland. The man, Arthur John Gossip, pastor of the Beechgrove Church. He was fifty-four years old and at the height of his powers.

Historians tell us that he was a humble and sincere man, possessing a keen wit and deeply devoted to his family and friends. A bit of an eccentric, he sometimes scandalized his staid Scottish congregation by appearing in public with a floppy fisherman's hat perched on his head. He is remembered as a man of strong opinions who never held back from expressing them to any and all who cared to listen. And, finally, history tells us that he was beloved as a pastor and preacher.

In fact, he is remembered as a preacher primarily for one

particular sermon he preached in 1927. Widely regarded as one of the greatest ever preached, it was the first sermon he delivered after the sudden death of his wife. He titled his message "But When Life Tumbles In, What Then?" In it, he struggled to reconcile his Christian faith with the loss of a loved one.

These are his words:

> I do not understand this life of ours. But still less can I comprehend how people in trouble and loss and bereavement can fling away peevishly from the Christian faith. In God's name, fling to what? Have we not lost enough without losing that too?

How right he was. "So many people's religion is a fair-weather affair," as he put it. "A little rain, and it runs and crumbles; a touch of strain, and it snaps." But if we turn from faith in the time of trouble, what shall we turn to? Have we not lost enough without losing that too?

THE QUESTION OF THE AGES

Let us begin our journey together by spending some time in the book of Job, chapter 1. That is not the only place we could begin, but it makes sense to start there, because Job deals with timeless questions of suffering and loss. Even though the story is four thousand years old, it could have been written yesterday. Most of the book of Job is poetry, and the book has been properly called the greatest poem in all human history. As one writer said, "[It] bears the stamp of uncommon genius."

The book abounds with mysteries: Who wrote it? When? Where? Why? But the greatest mystery is found in the subject matter itself—the mystery of undeserved suffering. Why do bad things happen to good people? For centuries thoughtful people have pondered that question. Why do babies die? Why are innocent people held hostage by madmen? Why are the righteous passed over for promotion while the wicked seem to get away with murder?

The book does not answer those questions with a theory. It answers them with a story. We are invited to examine one man whose life tumbled in around him. Why did that happen and what did he do about it?

THE MAN WHO HAD IT ALL

The book of Job has a terse, direct, simple beginning. It unfolds likes film running at hyperspeed. The frames zip by one after the other as an entire life is squeezed into a handful of sentences.

The first five verses tell us three things about Job.

He Was a Righteous Man

"In the land of Uz there lived a man whose name was Job. This man was blameless and upright; he feared God and shunned evil" (Job 1:1). You could talk for hours about those four phrases: blameless, upright, fearing God, shunning evil. But suffice it to say that Job was as good a man as you will find in all the Bible.

He Was a Rich Man

"He had seven sons and three daughters, and he owned seven thousand sheep, three thousand camels, five hundred yoke of oxen and five hundred donkeys, and had a large number of servants. He was the greatest man among all the people of the East" (vv. 2–3).

It is hard to know how to translate this sentence into today's terms. I thought of Donald Trump or Ross Perot or Bill Gates, but they don't fit the image. Maybe I could say it this way. When *USA Today* printed a list of the world's billionaires several years ago, the number one family on the list was from the Middle East. Its net worth was something like $32 billion, mostly from oil-related investments. By spelling out the details about the sheep and camels and oxen and donkeys, our text is telling us that if a list of the world's richest people had been printed four thousand years ago, Job would have been at the top.

He Was a Religious Man

"His sons used to take turns holding feasts in their homes, and they would invite their three sisters to eat and drink with them. When a period of feasting had run its course, Job would send and have them purified. Early in the morning he would sacrifice a burnt offering for each of them, thinking, 'Perhaps my children have sinned and cursed God in their hearts.' This was Job's regular custom" (vv. 4–5). Here is that rarest of all rare creatures: A truly wealthy man who loves God more than he loves his money. Not only that, but a father who takes responsibility for the spiritual welfare of his own family.

The point of these first few verses is very clear: By the world's standards, Job was successful; by God's standards, he was righteous. Here is a man who truly had it all. He was wealthy *and* godly *and* popular. You couldn't find a person who would say a bad word about Job. I repeat what I said earlier—He is as good a man as you will find in all the Bible.

That fact is absolutely crucial to understanding his story. Let me say it carefully: *What happened to him happened because he was a good man!* Nothing in the book of Job makes sense unless that is true. Job is a case study in the suffering of the righteous. As hard as it may be to understand, it was his righteousness and his prosperity that brought on his enormous suffering. And yet the suffering was undeserved in the truest sense of the word.

ENTER SATAN

While you ponder that, consider what happens next. The story suddenly shifts to Job's first test. The scene changes from earth to heaven. Job never knew about this part. While he was on the earth tending to his vast holdings, Satan was having a conversation with God:

> One day the angels [the Hebrew calls them "the sons of God"] came to present themselves before the Lord, and Satan [the name means "accuser," and Satan will now live up to his name] also came with them. The Lord said to Satan, "Where have you come from?"
>
> Satan answered the Lord, "From roaming through the earth and going back and forth in it." (vv. 6–7)

This passage answers a prevailing misconception about Satan. If you ask the average Christian, "Where is Satan today?" most will say that Satan is in hell. But the Bible does not teach that. If Satan were in hell today, we would have no problems at all. As Hal Lindsey put it a few years ago, "Satan is alive and well on planet earth." In this age, the earth is under his power and domination. Thank God, the day will come when Satan and all his hordes will be cast into the lake of fire forever (Matthew 25:41; Revelation 20:10). But that won't happen until Jesus returns to the earth. Between now and then, Satan roams about on the earth like a roaring lion, seeking men and women he can devour (1 Peter 5:8).

Since that is true, I take with utter seriousness the rising tide of Satanism in America today. It is one more sign that we are living in the last days.

Let us be perfectly clear. There is a personal being called Satan who once was an angel of God but who rebelled and fell from heaven to earth. In that rebellion he led one-third of the angels with him. Those fallen angels became the demons. From the day of his fall until now, Satan has had but one purpose: to frustrate God's plan by seeking to destroy men and women on the earth. After all these thousands of years, Satan is still at it.

I say all of that to make the point that Satan was behind

what happened to Job. Job never knew that and God never told him, but the writer of the book lets us peek behind the heavenly curtain to see the unfolding drama.

Satan Is Not the Issue

That brings us to the key passage. Notice in verse 8 that it is God who brings Job's name up. "Have you considered my servant Job? There is no one on earth like him." That's the other side of the coin. Satan was behind Job's trials, but God was behind Satan. It's not Satan who brings Job up. It's God.

It is as if God were saying, "All right, Satan, you're looking for a good man. Let me tell you about Job. He's the best man I've got. I don't think you can break him down."

What an insight that is. Behind the suffering is Satan, and behind Satan is God. That is why, as you read the book of Job, you find that Job is complaining bitterly against God. He never brings up Satan. Satan is not the issue. God is.

Even though Satan was the one who caused the calamity, he did so with God's permission. If God had not given his permission, Satan could not have touched a hair of Job's head.

Does Job Serve God for Nothing?

In verse 9 we come to the key question of the book: "Does Job fear God for nothing?" Satan is accusing God of bribing Job into worshiping Him. After all, Job has it all: a huge, loving family, enormous wealth, a great reputation— everything in this world a man could want. No wonder he worships God. Who wouldn't?

That's what Satan means when he says in verse 10, "Have you not put a hedge around him?" You gave him all of that and then you protect him from anything that could harm him. He's living on easy street; he doesn't have a worry in the world. Big deal. Of course he's your best man. He's also your richest man. You do take care of your own, don't you?

Behind it all is a not-so-subtle message. You've bribed him with prosperity. You dangle riches in front of him like a carrot on a stick. Satan is accusing God of rigging the system. It's as if there were a contract between Job and God that went like this:

I'll be good, and You will bless me.
I'll be pious, and You will give me prosperity.

Satan is attacking Job's motive and God's integrity. Here is the real question of the book of Job: *Will anyone serve God for no personal gain?*

Satan says the answer is no. Job will worship God only when things are going his way. Thus he says in verse 11: "But stretch out your hand and strike everything he has, and he will surely curse you to your face."

Satan's question is the supreme question of life. You served God in the sunshine; will you now serve Him in the shadows? You believed Him in the light of day; will you still believe Him at midnight? You sang His praises when all was going well; will you still sing through your tears? You came to church and declared, "The Lord is my Shepherd. I shall not want." Is He still your shepherd in the valley of the shadow of death?

He was good enough for you when you had money in the bank. Is He good enough for you when you have no money at all? He was good enough for you when you had your health. Is He good enough when the doctor says, "You have six months to live"? He was good enough when you were married. Is He good enough when the one you love walks out on you? He was good enough when your family was all together. Is He good enough when you stand around an open grave?

It's not hard to believe in God when everything is going your way. Anyone can do that. But when life tumbles in, what then?

FOUR MESSENGERS OF MISFORTUNE

Now the scene shifts from heaven to earth. Satan has received God's permission to put Job to the test. Notice that it happens on a "day when Job's sons and daughters were feasting and drinking wine at the oldest brother's house" (v. 13). In a moment of great happiness, at a family reunion, when you would least expect it, Satan strikes.

First, the Sabeans steal Job's livestock and kill his servants (vv. 14–15).

Second, a "fire of God" destroys his sheep and kills his servants (v. 16).

Third, the Chaldeans steal his camels and kill his servants (v. 17).

Fourth, a great wind hits the house where his children are feasting and kills them all (vv. 18–19).

The four messengers of misfortune come to Job one after another. Three times the text says, "While he was still speaking" (vv. 16, 17, 18). In the space of a few minutes, Job lost everything that was dear to him. His vast wealth: vanished. His empire: crumbled. His workers: murdered. His children: killed.

That's the worst of it. When tragedy strikes, it often comes again and again. And we think, *This must be the worst of it.* Then comes another knock at the door. Just when it seems that things can't get any more terrible, the bottom falls out again.

370 AND RISING

Have you ever taken one of those tests designed to measure the stress in your life? Typically, the test lists some fifty stress-producing events and assigns a numerical score to each event. Some events have a relatively low point value:

Moving to a new home: 20 points
Trouble with in-laws: 29 points

Others produce much more stress:

Divorce: 73 points
Death of a spouse: 100 points

You simply check off the events that have happened to you in the last twelve months and then total up the points. According to the test, if your total score for a year is from 0 to 150, you have only a 37 percent chance of undergoing a severe mental or emotional crisis in the next two years. If your score is from 150 to 300, the probability rises to 51 percent. But if your score is over 300, there is an 80 percent probability that you will soon face a severe mental or emotional crisis. The stress level in your life is simply too high.

Something like that happened to me in 1974. That was the year the bottom fell out of my life. Within a period of less than six months, I got engaged, graduated from college, took a new job, went on a long trip, got married, moved to a new state, started seminary, and then, two months later, experienced the death of my father. My score on the stress scale was up to 370—and rising.

By the end of the year I was a basket case. Everything good was bitter to me. I hated life. It had been too much to take.

But Job lost it all—not in a year or in six months or in a couple of weeks, but in a single afternoon. That teaches a solemn lesson—that tragedy is no respecter of persons. You can be on top of the world and lose it all in the twinkling of an eye. Tragedy can come to the same house again and again, and there is nothing to do to stop it.

FROM WEEPING TO WORSHIP

The only thing that is left is to see Job's response.

There Is Genuine Sorrow

"At this, Job got up and tore his robe and shaved his head" (v. 20). These are the actions of a man whose heart has been torn apart. They are public symbols of inner pain, much like wearing black to a funeral.

Some Christians think it is wrong to grieve over a great loss. They believe that tears somehow show a lack of faith in God. Even in a great loss, they believe it is somehow holy to put up a good front and never show pain. They even have trouble dealing with people who show great emotion after a severe loss.

I remember discussing this with a friend who told me that when his father died he never cried, not even once. He simply called the undertaker, and that was that. When I told him that I had cried many times in thinking about my father's death, he simply could not understand it. To him, tears were a sign of weakness.

But the Bible never says that. We are told that "Jesus wept" (John 11:35). Abraham and David and Jeremiah were real flesh-and-blood men who were not afraid to weep and cry and cover themselves with mourning garments. No one believed in God more than they did, and yet they were not ashamed to let others see their pain.

We do not have a high priest who cannot be touched with our weaknesses (see Hebrews 4:15). Jesus knows what we're going through because He was here with us. He knows what it's like to die of a broken heart. If our Lord was not ashamed of His tears, we shouldn't be ashamed of ours.

Job Worships God

"Then he fell to the ground in worship" (Job 1:20). Here is the ultimate response of the man of faith in the face of unexplainable tragedy. He weeps and then he worships. This is what differentiates the Christian from the rest of the world. They weep; we weep. They get angry; we worship. Our sorrow is just as real as theirs, but their sorrow leads only to despair, whereas ours leads to worship.

NAKED I CAME, NAKED I GO

Verse 21 records Job's great statement of faith. He says three things.

1. "Naked I came from my mother's womb, and naked I will depart."

This is literally true, as every husband who has ever been present in the delivery room can testify. All babies are born naked. We have a phrase for that. We say that a naked person is wearing his "birthday suit." But it's just as true at the end of life. We leave the way we enter. We bring nothing with us, and we take nothing with us. Sometimes when a person dies we ask, "How much did he leave?" The answer is always the same: "He left it all." The Italian proverb says, "The last robe has no pockets." In the words of Billy Graham, "You'll never see a Brinks truck following a hearse." When you die, you leave it all behind.

All we have is given to us on temporary loan. No matter how much we have been given in this life, we cannot keep it. In the end we have to give it back.

2. "The Lord gave and the Lord has taken away."

This is the man of faith speaking. This statement rises above the first one. It is true that we leave it all behind. But the man of faith understands that all we have we never owned in the first place. All that we have was given to us by God. He can take what is rightfully His any time He wants. Because He is God, He doesn't have to ask our permission before He takes it back, nor does He have to explain Himself afterward.

3. "May the name of the Lord be praised."

Job's faith now rises to its highest level. He has lost it all: his wealth, his workers, his children. All that he counted dear in life has been ripped from his grasp. Yet in the midst of his pain, Job praises God.

Here is the great point: *Job draws his argument for praise from the bitterness of suffering.* His loss drives him back to the goodness of God. Every pain is a reminder of how good God has been to him.

Someone has said that "the magnitude of the loss determines the size of the gift." The greater the sorrow, the greater the joy must have been. Every tear is a way of saying, "Thank you, Lord, for what you gave me." In Job's case, the more he grieves, the more he blesses the name of the Lord.

FOUR SIMPLE CONCLUSIONS

Our text ends with these amazing words: "In all this, Job did not sin by charging God with wrongdoing" (v. 22). He didn't ask why, he didn't accuse God of not loving him, he didn't claim his rights, he didn't curse God, and he didn't give up his faith. He simply said to himself, *If God takes something away from me, I will thank Him that I had it to enjoy for just a little while.*

As I ponder this remarkable story, four conclusions come to mind.

1. Undeserved suffering often comes to righteous men and women.

This is surely an obvious lesson, and although we have heard it before, we need to hear it again. Three times the text emphasizes that Job was a righteous man. What happened to him did not happen because of any moral fault or hidden sin in his life. It is a human tendency when tragedy strikes to believe that if we had only lived a better life the tragedy would never have happened. Sometimes that is true, but more often it is not. If the story of Job teaches us anything, it is that sometimes the most godly people suffer the most unexplainable losses. We will return to this point in later chapters, but let us nail it down in our thinking. Terrible things sometimes *do* happen to good people.

2. God is the source and owner of all you have.

God is the ultimate source of all that you have, and He has the absolute right to take that which belongs to Him. Your house? It is His. Your job? It is His. Your future? It is His. Your health? It is His. Your children? Yes, even your children are His. They belonged to Him before they ever belonged to you. Your husband or your wife? Yes, even your husband or your wife. All that you have belongs to God. And in the end, you will give it all back to Him. Sometimes He will take back something sooner than you would like to give it. But that is His absolute right, for He is God.

3. Your personal trials relate to God's purpose for your life.

Your personal trials can never be caused by blind fate or bad luck. They all somehow relate to God's purpose for your life. If this were not true, the Bible would not be true. If you don't come to believe this, you will eventually give up your faith. When tragedy strikes, the tendency is to search for a cause, a reason, an explanation, a chain of events stretching back into the past that would explain the catastrophe you now face. But as you search for causes, you will go back, and back, and back, until at last you come to God. And, as I say, if you do not eventually conclude that what happens to you somehow flows from God's loving purpose for your life, you will sooner or later give up your faith altogether.

4. Trials are designed to draw you nearer to God.

The one great biblical purpose for trials is to draw you

nearer to God. The question is not, "Why did this happen to me?" The deeper question is, "Now that this has happened, will I remain loyal to God?"

"WHAT ALTERNATIVE DO YOU PROPOSE?"

And that brings us back to A. J. Gossip's sermon and the great question, "When life tumbles in, what then?" If we turn away from our faith in times of trouble, what shall we turn to? Have we not lost enough without losing that too? When life crashes in against us and all that we value most is taken from us, if we then give up our faith, where will we go and what will we do?

Pastor Gossip said these words in his sermon: "You people in the sunshine *may* believe the faith, but we in the shadow *must* believe it. We have nothing else."

Stephen Brown tells about a seminar one of his associate pastors was leading. During one session, the associate pastor said that because God is love, no matter how bad things get, Christians should praise Him. Afterward, a man came up to him in great agitation. "Dave, I can't buy it. I can't buy what you say about praising God in the midst of evil and hurt." Then he went on to say what many people secretly feel. "I do not believe that when you lose someone you love through death, or you have cancer, or you lose your job, that you ought to praise God." After a moment's silence, the associate pastor replied very simply, "What alternative do you propose?"

We do not gain if we turn away from God in the time of trouble. If we turn away from God, we lose our only ground of hope.

JEFF HUGHES

Jeff Hughes graduated from Southwestern Baptist Theological Seminary in Fort Worth, Texas, in 1984. Like hundreds of other graduates, he looked forward to serving the

Lord as a pastor. He was twenty-eight-years-old, and had received valuable training for the work. But there was one difference. Jeff Hughes was dying of cancer. It had been discovered in March; he graduated in May. Two churches told him they could not call a man they knew would soon be dead. But the Mount Nebo Baptist Church in Lockwood, Missouri, felt differently.

On May 13 the church called him to become their pastor. He had a wonderful time there. The people took him into their hearts. At one point Jeff told his wife Pat, "The Lord is either going to heal me or He's being very good to me in my last days."

The congregation has not forgotten those few brief weeks. Donna Watson, one of the members, said, "He loved everybody and everybody loved him." Then she said, "He never once was angry at God; he was angry at cancer. He never once doubted the Lord and His love. He had questions, just as anyone would, but he kept thinking of others or of Pat or of the church."

Another man said, "He was surely a witness for the Lord. He had as much faith as any man I've ever known." The last two Sundays he preached from a wheelchair.

Jeff Hughes died of cancer of the pancreas on August 13, 1984. He worked as a pastor until the very end. One of the members said, "There's no way to tell how many people were influenced by him."

CORDS STRONGER THAN STEEL

As A. J. Gossip came to the end of his sermon, he said, "I don't think you need to be afraid of life. Our hearts are very frail; and there are places where the road is very steep and very lonely. But we have a wonderful God."

Indeed we do. And as the apostle Paul puts it, what can separate us from the love of God? Nothing at all. Not life, nor death, nor tragedy, nor heartbreak, nor suffering. *We are forev-*

er connected to His love with cords a thousand times stronger than steel.

The question remains. When life tumbles in, what then? Through our tears, we go on believing. Our confidence rests in this: That He who brought us this far will take us safely home.

2

THE BLESSING
NO ONE WANTS

B lessed are those who mourn, for they will be comforted" (Matthew 5:4).

This is one of the strangest statements in the Bible. It is a paradox and a mystery. "Blessed are those who mourn," said Jesus. Happy are the sad! What do these strange words mean? Who are the mourners, why are they sad, and how are they comforted?

I learned something about this beatitude during one long week a few months ago. On Monday I spent all day at Rush Presbyterian-St. Luke's Hospital in Chicago, arriving about nine in the morning and leaving sometime after six that night. My wife and I sat in the waiting room during a friend's nine-hour cancer surgery. As we waited for news from the operating room, it occurred to me that this was the longest time I had spent in any hospital since my father died twenty-three years ago. My friend Len had been diagnosed with cancer only a few weeks earlier. He was only forty-two years old. At his request, we prayed for a miracle of divine healing so that he would not have to go through the surgery, but that request was not granted. But God did spare him through the surgery, which in its own way was a gracious miracle.

That was only the beginning of the week. On Wednesday morning I conducted a funeral service for another forty-two-year-old man who had just died of liver cancer. Although many of us prayed for Mike, most people did it by faith because he came to the church I pastor less than three years ago, and for the past year his cancer had made it difficult for him to attend services.

I'll never forget the first time I met him. We were having the Wednesday night Bible study in the chapel, and one evening a nice-looking couple walked in. I had no idea who they were. When I asked if anyone would like prayer for healing, Mike came forward. He told us that he had just been diagnosed with cancer. It was hard to believe because he was a big, well-built fellow. I'll never forget his reaction when I asked him if he wanted to say anything before we prayed for him. With tears rolling down his face, he said, "I've been away from the Lord for a while, but I'm coming back tonight. And whether God heals me or not, I'm going to dedicate my life to Him no matter how long I live."

WE HAVEN'T LOST HIM

Mike and I talked many times over the next two years. A few months before his death I dropped by to see him at home. It was clear that the end was near. Cancer had reduced him to a shell of the man he had once been. But he was still smiling. As he sat in his rocking chair, we started talking about what it's like to die. I told him about heaven and gave him the promise of God that to be absent from the body is to be present with the Lord. And I did something that afternoon that I have never done any other time. I told him what I was going to say at his funeral service. It only seems fair that the guest of honor should know what is being said about him.

Basically, I told him that I was going to tell the mourners about his rededication to Jesus Christ and how he had died as a Christian and gone to heaven according to the Lord's own promise.

About a month later I had the privilege of going to Mike's home and serving him his last communion. Then one night his wife called and asked me to come over because he was fading fast. I got there about 10:30. I held his hand, and we talked about heaven. "Mike, you don't have a thing to worry about. When you die, you are going directly into the presence of Jesus Christ. Before Barb can get to the phone to call me, you will already be in heaven."

His funeral that Wednesday morning was a triumphant affair. When my time came to speak, I kept my promise to Mike and said exactly what I had told him I was going to say. And I told the mourners not to say, "We've lost Mike." That's not right. A thing is lost only when you don't know where it is. Mike's not lost. We know exactly where he is. He's in heaven.

Then I came to the Wednesday night supper and picked up the prayer list. It seemed to have a record number of sick people on it. I was struck by the fact that I didn't know almost half of the names on the list.

GOD DOESN'T LEAVE A TRAIL

That Sunday morning I told my congregation that I had been pondering all that had happened during the week. Why does one man live and another man die? Why does one person get sick and his brother stay healthy? Two men riding in a jeep roll over a mine. One is spared; the other loses a leg.

My friend Peter Blakemore died not long ago. I saw him for the last time when I attended a pastor's prayer meeting in connection with the National Day of Prayer. I came a few minutes late and found the men gathered in a circle ready to pray. As I walked in, I recognized most of the pastors immediately, except for one man in a wheelchair who was facing away from me. He had two teenaged boys by his side.

When I sat down, I realized the man in the wheelchair was Peter Blakemore, pastor of the Harrison Street Bible Church in Oak Park, Illinois. Peter was about forty years old, married, with seven wonderful children. He had lived in Oak Park all his life, the only exception being the years he was in college and graduate school. His father pastored the Harrison Street Bible Church for over thirty years, and then Peter took up the ministry in his father's stead.

Strange Pain

It all started when Peter noticed a strange pain in his pelvic area. When it wouldn't go away, he sought medical help, but the doctors couldn't pinpoint the source of trouble. Eventually they found a tumor, performed a biopsy, and sent it off for analysis. It took a long time to get a correct answer, but in due course, a lab on the West Coast reported that Peter had contracted a rare form of cancer. He began chemotherapy in a desperate attempt to eradicate it.

Nothing seemed to work. At one point Peter traveled to Dallas to investigate several specialized treatments. Those didn't work either.

When I saw Peter at the prayer meeting, he was bent over a bit, but smiling as he sat in the wheelchair. As we prayed, I heard a strange noise coming from my left. It was Peter's eldest son, rubbing his Dad's back because the pain was so intense.

A Face Radiant with God's Glory

I think Peter was the last one to pray. He said something like this: "Lord, when I discovered I had cancer, the only thing I asked was that you might use this to honor and glorify your name. I thank you, Lord, that you have abundantly answered my prayer. If I make it, I will stand up and give you praise. But if I don't, I'll give you honor and glory till the very end."

As soon as the prayer meeting broke up, I sat down beside Peter and asked him how he was doing. He smiled as he told me the story. The news was not good. A tumor had developed in his right lung, growing to the point that it had shattered several of his ribs. That was why he was doubled over in pain.

Peter told me that the doctors did not know for sure what kind of cancer this new tumor was. They told him that it could be one of two kinds. "If it is one kind," he said, "I have two or three weeks to live. If it's the other kind, then I have one or two months."

He said it calmly, without fear or panic. In fact, he was smiling as he said it. As I looked at him, his face was radiant with the glory of God. Like Moses of old, my friend Peter had seen the Lord, and now nothing else mattered.

He told me that he preached the previous Sunday for the first time in seven weeks. They had to prop him up in his wheelchair, but he somehow found the strength to preach for an hour from Romans 11:33, "His paths [are] beyond tracing out." That text means that you can't trace God's footsteps. You don't know where He's come from, and you can't tell where He is going. All you know is that He is with you in the midst of your pain.

Still Smiling

The room was empty. All the other pastors were gone. Peter's last words to me were these: "All my life I've been speaking about God's grace and trying to get people to listen. Now they listen when I speak, because I've discovered that through it all, God's grace is sufficient."

With that, his sons began to wheel him from the room. Though bent over with pain, he smiled and waved at me as he left.

The words of Paul came to my mind, "Though outwardly we are wasting away, yet inwardly we are being renewed day by day" (2 Corinthians 4:16).

Why did my friend Peter die so young when he had so much to offer the world?

It is a mystery hidden in the mind and heart of God. All human explanations must ultimately fail. "The secret things belong to the Lord our God" (Deuteronomy 29:29). Is there an answer to the question Why? Yes, there is, but the answer is hidden from our view.

To all our questions, God replies, "I AM WHO I AM" (Exodus 3:14). The answer is a Person, not an explanation. Someone may reply, "But that's not enough. I want a real answer." To which I reply, "If God Himself is not enough, then no answer would ever satisfy you."

THE MINISTRY OF DIVINE COMFORT

But to leave the matter there would not be fair, for the Bible has a great deal to say about the ministry of divine comfort. It tells us a number of important truths we need to remember.

1. God Himself draws near to those who hurt.

Psalm 34:18 says, "The Lord is close to the brokenhearted and saves those who are crushed in spirit." Here is a promise of God's special presence in the midst of our pain. Through the Holy Spirit, the Lord himself draws near to us in times of great suffering. We sense His presence in a way that goes beyond the natural. We hear His voice though there is no sound in the room. Many Christians can testify to this special sense of God's nearness felt during a time of great suffering.

2. God uses suffering to draw us to Himself.

In this same Psalm David declared, "I sought the Lord, and he answered me; he delivered me from all my fears" (v. 4). Suffering turns us to the Lord as nothing else can. I think it was Ron Dunn who said, "You never know if Jesus is all you need until Jesus is all you have. And when Jesus is all you have, then and only then will you discover that Jesus really is all you need." We pray more, and we pray more fervently during a time of crisis because we know that if God doesn't help us, we're sunk. Sometimes I think that God allows certain things to happen to His children in order to get our attention focused completely on Him.

3. We grow faster in hard times than we do in good times.

Romans 5:2–4 describes the process God uses to develop godly character in our lives. In fact, Paul says that "we also rejoice in our sufferings" (v. 3). That may appear to be a misprint, but it isn't. Paul isn't suggesting that we should become masochists who rejoice in the hard times as if we enjoyed the pain. That wouldn't even be a Christian idea. He doesn't say, "We rejoice *because of* our sufferings" but rather, "We rejoice *in* our sufferings."

Even in the most difficult moments, God's people can rejoice because He is at work doing something important in them. The next few verses explain the process. Suffering produces perseverance, perseverance produces character, character produces hope, and "hope does not disappoint us." Why is that, Paul? "Because God has poured out his love into our hearts by the Holy Spirit" (v. 5). What starts with suffering ends with the love of God. This is a wonderful progression, but you cannot get to the love of God without starting in the place of suffering.

More than one person has said to me, "I wouldn't trade my pain for the things God has shown me." If that doesn't make sense to you, it is only because you haven't been there yet.

4. Our sufferings qualify us to minister to others.

Second Corinthians 1:4 tells us that God "comforts us in

all our troubles, so that we can comfort those in any trouble with the comfort we ourselves have received from God." The Greek word translated "comfort" in this verse is the same word Jesus used in Matthew 5:4. God uses our sufferings to comfort us so that when we are better, we can then minister to others in His name.

During that long week that never seemed to end, Mike's wife volunteered to sit with Len's wife in the hospital. She didn't even know Roberta, but she was willing to go. Why? Because no one understands cancer like someone who has been through it. No one understands divorce like a person who's been through it. No one understands the pain of a miscarriage like a mother who has lost a child that way. No one knows the pain of losing a job like someone who has lost a job.

Many Christians are superbly qualified to minister to others—and they don't even know it. They are the ones who have been deeply hurt by the troubles of life—and, through it all, they have discovered that God is faithful. Those folks have an important message to share. They can say with conviction, "God will take care of you. I know, because He took care of me."

They have earned their degree in the School of Suffering, and now they are qualified to minister to others who are newly enrolled.

The Majesty of God's Sovereignty

What do these things teach us about the character of God?

1. Because God is sovereign and we are not, most of our questions will never be answered in this life.

Some people can't live with that truth, so they devise human answers to explain suffering and death. Those answers almost never work, and sometimes they hurt more than they help. When I am called to the hospital, I never try to answer these hard questions. They are beyond me. Better to say less and be silent before the Lord than to try to explain the mysterious ways of God.

2. Because God is good, we know that He has our best interests at heart.

That in one sentence is the meaning of Romans 8:28. The older I get, the more I am convinced that the goodness of God is the central issue of life. If you believe God is good, you can endure things that would break most people. You can live with unanswered questions so long as you believe in the goodness of God. But once you doubt His goodness, you must become either a secret atheist or an angry Christian. And really, there's not much difference in those two categories, if you think about it.

In stating it that way, it is important to remember that God's goodness doesn't depend on our happiness. A few months ago our son and a few friends survived a late-night wreck that totally destroyed our new van. The man at the local body shop estimated that when the van hit the tree it was going at least fifty miles per hour. The force of the impact drove the engine eighteen inches off its block and into the passenger compartment. You could see tufts of hair in the windshield left from the force of the impact. In the providence of God, the van hit the tree in the center of the front bumper. "If it had hit the tree six inches to the left or right, you would have been going to the funeral home, not to the hospital," the man told us.

It was a miracle that I cannot explain. At one point that night, there were four people in four different hospitals. But no one died, and we eventually replaced our van. Several months later, during a Thanksgiving service, my wife rose to give a testimony. She said something like this: "Many of you know that our oldest son and his friends barely survived a terrible wreck. And some people have told us that God was good to spare Joshua and the others who were with him. It's true that God was good to us, but God would have been good even if Joshua had died in the wreck."

I confess that I was unnerved when I heard those words. Like many people, I am accustomed to connecting God's goodness with my happiness. But it doesn't work that way. I listened to Eddie Fox describe what happens in the Methodist churches of Nigeria. He said that whenever the church gathers, the speaker will say, "Hallelujah," and everyone responds, "Amen." When the speaker says, "God is good," with one voice they reply, "All the time."

Our Nigerian brothers and sisters are right. God is good all the time.

God's character is not on trial in your sufferings. You may think it is, but it isn't. Job tried to put God on trial, but the Lord ended up putting Job on trial.

God is good, and His mercy endures forever. That is true regardless of our moment-by-moment experience.

3. Because God is wise, nothing is ever wasted in our experience.

Romans 8:29 tells us that God has predestined us to be conformed to the image of Jesus Christ. I often think of a sculptor sitting down before a hunk of marble. On the outside, the marble looks ugly and unformed. But the sculptor sees something beautiful inside that hunk. So with hammer and chisel, he begins to chip away. For many weeks he shapes, cuts, and polishes, until little by little an image emerges from the stone. On and on he works, never stopping until the sculpture is complete. What was once ugly is now a thing of beauty.

Even so, the Lord God takes the hammer and chisel of human suffering to shape us into the image of Jesus Christ. And in those moments when we feel that God has simply hammered us into the ground, we discover later that nothing was done in anger, nothing in haste, but everything was according to His plan so that, in the end, we might be beautiful, like Jesus Himself.

I can testify that the most beautiful Christians I know are not the young, the rich, the educated, the successful, or the influential. Those persons may be happy, but their lives are shallow because the sculptor has not yet picked up the hammer and the chisel. *No, the most beautiful Christians I know are those who have been through suffering and come through it with their faith in God intact.* They may not laugh as much as others and their faces may be lined with care, but the beauty of Christ is in their eyes and their voices testify to God's amazing grace.

If you feel the heavy weight of God hammering down on you, rest assured that nothing is being wasted. Everything has a purpose. In the end, God will be glorified, and you will be more beautiful than you ever dreamed possible.

4. Because God is love, He will not leave you alone in your pain.

This is the promise of the second Beatitude, "Blessed are those who mourn, for they will be comforted" (Matthew 5:4). God will come to you. You may not feel it or believe it, but it is true, for He has promised it. If it were necessary, I could produce a long line of witnesses who could stand and testify to God's comfort in the midst of great suffering.

But it is not necessary to do that. I know God will come to you, because He came for you two thousand years ago. There's an old gospel song that contains the whole truth in just a few words:

> Out of the ivory palaces,
> Into a world of woe,
> Only His great eternal love
> Made my Savior go.
> —Henry Barraclough,
> "Ivory Palaces"[1]

God proved his love when He sent His Son Jesus into this sin-cursed world. He didn't have to do it. He chose to do it. He did what we would never do—He voluntarily sacrificed His only Son. He not only sent Him to earth, He stood by and watched Him die a terrible, bloody death.

After Calvary, God has nothing left to prove to anyone. How can you doubt His love after you look at the bleeding form of Jesus hanging on the cross?

> See from His head, His hands, His feet,
> Sorrow and love flow mingled down;
> Did e'er such love or sorrow meet,
> Or thorns compose so rich a crown?
> —Isaac Watts,
> "When I Survey the Wondrous Cross"

I realize that this may not answer every question, but it does answer the most important question: Does God care for me in the midst of my suffering? The answer is yes, God cares for you—and if you doubt His love, look to the Cross and be comforted.

We understand these strange words a bit better when we see them refracted through the bloody haze of Good Friday. See Him on the cross, "a man of sorrows, and acquainted with grief" (Isaiah 53:3 KJV). He knows what you are going through; He will personally comfort you; and in the end, you will be blessed.

NOTES

1. Henry Barraclough, "Ivory Palaces." Copyright 1915. Renewal, 1943, by H. Barraclough. Assigned to and Arr. Copyright, © 1957, by Hope Publishing Company. International Copyright secured. All rights reserved.

3

THE MYSTERY OF UNANSWERED PRAYER

The man stood over my desk and said, "You won't believe the things that have happened to me." Then he proceeded to tell a tale of woe the likes of which I had not heard in many years. As I listened, it seemed to boil down to three basic parts. First, he had lost his promising career through a complicated series of cunning plots against him. Then his wife left him for greener pastures and more security. And now he was facing a veritable mountain of legal bills. He seemed to be backed into a corner. His question was simple: Why would God let something like this happen to me?

The phone rang about nine o'clock one night. The voice at the other end said, "Pastor Pritchard, could I talk to you for a few minutes?" As I listened, I heard a story about a marriage gone bad. She had married him a few years ago, and things had not gone well. He abused her, and later on he abused the kids. Eventually she filed for divorce, and now he wants nothing to do with her or the children. In her heart of hearts, her greatest desire is for God to give her someone to be a loving husband and godly father. She has prayed and prayed about it, but there seems to be no answer. "Pastor Pritchard, why doesn't God answer my prayers? Is He punishing me because I got a divorce?"

The message said that I needed to go to Methodist Central Hospital in Dallas. Lois McCallum had been taken there in an ambulance. Buddy and Lois were dear friends, an older couple who faithfully attended my Sunday school class. That morning Lois had awakened with a headache that quickly deteriorated into something much worse. The paramedics suspected a stroke. By the time I got to the hospital the diagnosis was confirmed. Lois couldn't talk, but she could squeeze my hand. "Lois, this is Pastor Ray. Do you recognize me?" She did. I prayed for her, and then I said, "Lois, don't worry. You're going to be all right. We're going to pray you through this." We did pray—the whole church prayed—but things weren't all right. That night she had another stroke, this time a massive hemorrhage that left her comatose. Five days later she died. In the end, our prayers seemed to make no difference.

In the last chapter I told about two forty-two-year-old men with cancer. My friend Len survived nine hours of surgery only to die of a blood clot in the lungs nine days later. He had been an elder of our church, was greatly beloved, and had been prayed for so hard and so long. Why did God bring him through the surgery only to let him die a few days later?

WHERE IS GOD WHEN WE NEED HIM?

Of all the things that weigh us down, perhaps no burden is greater than the silence of God.

- A godly mother prays for her wayward son. He was raised in the church, he went to Sunday school, he knows the Bible—but when he left home, he left it all behind. For many years his mother has prayed for him, but to this day he remains a prodigal son.

- A wife prays for her husband, who left her after twenty-three years of marriage for a younger woman. He seems utterly unreachable, and the marriage heads swiftly for divorce.

- A husband prays for his wife, who has terminal cancer. She has six, maybe seven months to live. None of the treatments stop the rampaging tumors. The elders anoint her with oil and pray over her in the name of the Lord. She dies five months later.

- A young man prays fervently for deliverance from an overpowering temptation, but the struggle never seems to end. The more he prays, the worse the temptation becomes.

And so we cry out with the psalmist, "Why, O Lord, do you stand far off? Why do you hide yourself in times of trouble?" (Psalm 10:1).

THE PROBLEM NO ONE TALKS ABOUT

As we think about this question we will be helped if we simply acknowledge reality. *A great many believers struggle with the issue of unanswered prayer.* If there is a God, if He really does answer prayer, why doesn't He answer my prayers?

For those who are in pain, a theoretical answer will not suffice. Nor will it be enough to simply say, "God always answers prayer. Sometimes He says yes, sometimes He says no, and sometimes He says wait awhile." We say this a lot. I've said it myself. But it sounds facile and superficial when someone cries out to God from the pit of despair, and the heavens are as brass, and the answer never comes.

There are people who bear hidden scars from the pain of prayers that were not answered. They remember times when they prayed, really prayed, said all the right words with all the right motives, even asked their friends to join them in prayer, deeply believing that only God could help them out;

and after they prayed, they waited and waited and waited, but God never seemed to answer.

We don't talk about this problem very much. I suppose that's because we're afraid that if we admit our prayers aren't always answered, it will cause some people to lose their faith in God.

As a matter of fact, that's exactly what has happened. Many good, devout people secretly doubt that God answers prayer. They doubt it, for when it really counted, God did not come through for them. So in their hearts, deep in the inner recesses of the soul, hidden behind a smiling face, rests a profound disenchantment with the Almighty.

CALVIN AND HOBBES

You wouldn't think that such a serious subject would make it to the comic strips, but I happened to find it there some months ago. The comic strip was "Calvin and Hobbes." It's late November, and a little boy is waiting with his sled for the first big snowfall. He waits and waits—but all he finds is brown grass . . . and no snow.

So he says, "If I was in charge, we'd never see grass between October and May." Then, looking to the heavens, he says, "On 'three,' ready? One . . . Two . . . Three. SNOW!" Nothing happens, and the little boy is downcast. Then he shouts to the heavens, "I said snow! C'mon! Snow!" Then, shaking his fists, he cries, "SNOW!" Now thoroughly disgusted with God's failure, he says, "OK then, don't snow! See what I care! I like this weather! Let's have it forever!"

But his defiance does not last. In the next frame we see the little boy on his knees offering this prayer: "Please snow! Please?? Just a foot! OK, eight inches! That's all! C'mon! Six inches, even! How about just six??" Then he looks to heaven and shouts, "I'm WAAIITING . . ."

In the next frame we see him running in a circle, head

down, fists clenched, making a little-boy sound which the artist spells out as "RRRRGGHHH." That's not an English word, but every parent has heard it many times. Finally, the little boy is exhausted, his energy spent, his prayer unanswered, with snow nowhere in sight. In the final frame, he looks up at God and cries out in utter desperation, "Do you want me to become an atheist?"

Many Christian people feel just like that little boy, only they have prayed for things much more important than a few inches of snow—but the end result has been the same. And in their frustration and despair, they have cried out to God, "Do you want me to become an atheist?"

Some of them have. Most haven't, but they keep the pain inside, still believing as best they can in a God who sometimes answers prayer and sometimes doesn't.

MY OWN TESTIMONY

At this point I would like to add my own testimony to the list. Many years ago my father suddenly and inexplicably became very ill. I was just married and was starting seminary when I got the late-night call from my mom. My father was in the hospital and very sick. They had taken him to Birmingham. Marlene and I made the trip from Dallas, and the whole thing was like a dream to me. My dad was a doctor. Doctors don't get sick; they heal the sick. How could *my* dad be in the hospital? But he was, and the outlook was not good. Something about a strange bacterial infection that the doctors could not stop.

And so began a two-week ordeal I will never forget. We went to Birmingham and then back to Dallas. A few days later the call came and we went back again. This time Dad was worse. I prayed, but it was hard and I was scared.

I remember when the turning point came. It was on the second trip when I went in to see my father in intensive care. By this time, he was in and out of a coma, and I don't think he knew who I was. When I went back out in the hallway, I saw my boyhood friend, Neil Jones. He had come down to see how I was doing. Something about seeing an old friend triggered my emotions, and I collapsed against the wall and began to weep. It was in that terrible moment that I realized my father was dying, and I could do nothing about it.

A few days later, my father died despite our prayers and the doctors' best efforts. Twenty-three years have passed, and I know many things now that I didn't know then. I understand life a little better. But after all these years, I still don't know why God didn't answer our prayers. The mystery is as great to me today as it was in the hospital corridor in Birmingham, Alabama. I didn't know then, and I don't know now.

MY GRACE IS SUFFICIENT FOR THEE

But I have been helped by one great discovery: *I'm not the first person to have my prayers go unanswered.* In fact, the Bible is filled with stories of men and women who prayed to God in the moment of crisis, and God—for reasons sometimes explained and more often not explained—did not answer their prayers. We don't hear much about that because our focus is naturally on the great answers that came just in the nick of time. Most of us would rather hear about the parting of the Red Sea than about Trophimus being left sick at Miletus. Miracles that did happen are more encouraging than stories of miracles that almost happened.

As I flip through the pages of the Bible, I find no story of unanswered prayer that encourages me more than the account of Paul's unanswered prayer in 2 Corinthians 12.

You remember it, I'm sure. In that passage Paul reveals that fourteen years earlier he had been caught up into heaven and had seen things that no mortal man had ever seen before. It was the greatest experience of his life, and he never forgot what it was like. But when that great experience was over, something else happened to Paul that would change his whole perspective on life. Let him tell the story in his own words:

> To keep me from becoming conceited because of these surpassingly great revelations, there was given me a thorn in my flesh, a messenger of Satan, to torment me. (2 Corinthians 12:7)

Bible students are divided about what this verse really means. Some suggest that the "thorn in the flesh" was the fierce opposition Paul received from his Jewish opponents. Others suggest it was some kind of demonic oppression. Still others think that the thorn was a physical ailment that crippled Paul in some way and limited his effectiveness.

In one sense it really doesn't matter. The crucial point is that Paul prayed for God to remove the "thorn in his flesh" so that he could get on with his ministry. In fact he prayed not once but three times. And each time God said no.

Can you imagine that? The apostle Paul, probably the greatest Christian who ever lived, the man who introduced Christianity to Europe, the man who wrote so much of the New Testament—that man, when he prayed about this need in his life, found that God did not, *would* not, answer his prayers.

It's hard to believe because we know that Paul was a man of prayer. He writes about prayer in all his letters. Suppose the apostle were to come to your church next Sunday and after the service said, "Now, I'll be glad to pray for any of you." What would you do? I know what I'd do. I'd get in line and ask the apostle Paul to pray for me.

But here's a clear-cut case, given in his own words, of a time in his life when he desperately begged God over and over again to answer a very specific prayer, and God said no.

As I ponder this story, I gather great encouragement from it. It teaches me several important principles.

1. Unanswered prayer sometimes happens to the very best of Christians.

2. When it happens, it is humanly unexplainable.

3. When it happens, God has a higher purpose in mind.

In Paul's case he kept on praying until God finally gave him an explanation. "But he said to me, 'My grace is sufficient for you, for my power is made perfect in weakness'" (2 Corinthians 12:9).

Sometimes our prayers are not answered because God can do more through us by not answering our prayers than He can by answering them.

Sometimes God's no is better than His yes.

Think of it this way. What would happen if God answered all your prayers all the time in the exact manner in which you prayed? Forget for a moment that some of your prayers are foolish and shortsighted. Just suppose that God answered them all. Would that produce spiritual maturity in your life? I think not. If God always answered your prayers, eventually your trust would be in the answers and not in the Lord alone.

But when God says no, we are forced to decide whether we will still trust in God alone—without the benefit of an answered prayer to lean upon.

Don't get me wrong. Answered prayer is wonderful, and if *none* of our prayers were answered we would probably stop praying altogether. But if all of our prayers were answered we would end up taking God for granted. *Unanswered prayer forces us to trust in God alone.* And when we do, He alone gets the glory, for it is at that point that His strength is made perfect in our weakness.

"IF I WERE GOD, I WOULDN'T ANSWER THAT PRAYER"

While attending a seminar in a distant city, I ran into an old friend I hadn't seen in many years. The word had reached me that he had gone through a bitter divorce. Although I did not know all the details, I was aware that my friend had wandered from God.

I knew that much when I saw my old friend, but he didn't know I knew. When he saw me he came up and gave me a huge bear hug and said, "Ray, it's good to see you." We talked and agreed to meet for lunch the next day during a break between the conference sessions.

On Saturday we drove to a fast-food restaurant jammed with people from the conference. As we talked, my friend told me the whole sad story, a tale I had heard many times before. A young couple gets married in a burst of love and excitement. Children come along and the house is filled with diapers and toys. The husband is busy building his career; the wife takes care of the home. They are both so busy they hardly notice that somehow they have drifted apart.

In the beginning, church was a big part of their lives. They were learning, growing, making new friends. But later on they didn't have as much time, and eventually they just dropped out of sight.

Then came the affair. And eventually the divorce, and with it an avalanche of bitterness from his ex-wife. She wanted nothing to do with him, not now, not ever.

My friend admitted his guilt and confessed what a fool he had been. At some point after the divorce he hit bottom and began, at last, to look up. He cried out to God for help. He came back to the Lord and started going to church again. To anyone who would listen, he said, "All I want to do is put my marriage back together again."

As we ate lunch, I listened to my old friend pour out his heart. He couldn't understand why his ex-wife would not forgive him and take him back. "But now," he said, "I have come back to God, and I'm asking Him to put my marriage back together again." As I listened, I felt the intensity of his conviction and knew he really meant it.

We finished lunch and began to drive back to the conference. As we did, he repeated again that he was spending time in the Word and in prayer, asking God to give him his wife and children back again. When he said it, I looked at him and said, "If I were God, I wouldn't answer that prayer."

He looked at me as if I had lost my mind. "For the first time in years, God has you right where He wants you," I explained. "For a long time you took God for granted. You didn't pray, you didn't read the Word, you didn't seek His face when you made your decisions. You left God out of your life completely. And the result was that you lost the one thing that meant the most to you in all the world—your wife and your children. That's a heavy price to pay. But you've paid it.

"And now, after all that has happened, you are praying again. You are growing spiritually again. Knowing God has become the most important thing in your life. That's the way it should have been all along. Who's to say that if God answers your prayers too quickly you won't slip back into the old way of living? No, if I were God I wouldn't answer that prayer right now. I don't think it's in your best interest."

A Soldier's Prayer

Sometimes it is better for us if our prayers are not answered immediately. Sometimes it is better if they are not answered at all. The great question is not, "How can I get my prayers answered?" The great question is, "What will it take to draw me closer to God?"

At the end of a bloody battle during the Civil War, someone found the following prayer folded in the pocket of a dead Confederate soldier:

I asked God for strength, that I might achieve;
I was made weak, that I might learn humbly to obey.
I asked for health, that I might do greater things;

54

I was given infirmity, that I might do better things.
I asked for riches, that I might be happy;
I was given poverty, that I might be wise.
I asked for power, that I might have the praise of men;
I was given weakness, that I might feel the need of God.
I asked for all things, that I might enjoy life;
I was given life, that I might enjoy all things.
I got nothing I asked for, but everything I had hoped for.
Almost despite myself, my unspoken prayers were
    answered.
I am, among men, most richly blessed.

It is a great advance in spiritual understanding to be able to say, "I got nothing I asked for, but everything I had hoped for."

THOUGH HE SLAY ME

That brings me to the conclusion. Sometimes our prayers will go unanswered. Unless you admit that fact and deal with it as a Christian, you will probably give up prayer altogether. To make matters worse, sometimes our prayers offered from righteous motives and pure hearts will seem to accomplish nothing. It is as if the heavens have turned to brass.

But that is not true. God does hear every prayer, even the ones He chooses not to answer. And no prayer is entirely wasted, for even unanswered prayer may be used by God to draw us closer to Him. In that case we may say that it was better for our prayers to go unanswered that we might draw near to God.

The final solution, I think, lies somewhere along these lines: When we pray, we tend to focus exclusively on the answers; God wants us to focus on Him. Whatever will help us do that is what we really need. Sometimes that means our prayers will be answered in amazing and miraculous ways; other times our prayers will not be answered at all.

Do you remember the experience of Job? He lost his home, his fortune, his children, his health, and his reputation. All that he counted dear was taken away from him. When he finally hit the bottom, filled with anger and wishing that he were dead, he uttered these words of faith: "Though he slay me, yet will I trust in him" (Job 13:15 KJV).

"You can take my life, but you can't make me stop trusting in you." Yes, there is a note of belligerent defiance in those words, and yes, Job wasn't too happy about what God had done to him. And yes, he wanted his day in court. But underneath the anger and searing pain was a bedrock faith in God. "I don't understand this at all, but I'm hanging on to you, Lord, and I'm not going to let go."

That's the place to which God wants to bring us. Sometimes unanswered prayer is the only way to get us there.

WHAT TO DO WHEN YOUR PRAYERS ARE NOT ANSWERED

Having said all of that, we still need to know how to respond when we pray and God does not answer us. What do we do? I have three suggestions to make.

1. Keep on praying as long as you can.

Sometimes God's answers are delayed for reasons beyond our knowledge. Who can really say why a prayer which has been uttered 9,999 times should finally be answered the 10,000th time? But sometimes it happens.

From time to time we hear stories of how people have prayed for a loved one for twenty, and even thirty years, before the answer finally came. And we all know of stories of how some people have made miraculous recoveries after the doctors had given up all hope. Should not we gain hope from such seeming miracles?

Not long ago a woman stood up in a Sunday school class I was teaching and told about a friend (well-known to several others in our class) who had prayed for her husband's salvation for fifty-nine years. After all those years, he finally trusted Christ and died a few months later. Don't you think his wife must have gotten discouraged somewhere along the way? What if she had stopped praying after thirty-seven years?

So pray, pray, and keep on praying. And as you pray, don't be ashamed to beg God for a miracle. Who knows? You may be surprised to find that in the end, after you have given up all hope, God has moved from heaven to answer your prayers in ways you never dreamed possible.

2. Give God the right to say no to you.

In the larger sense, God already has that right, whether you acknowledge it or not. But if you never acknowledge that God has the right to say no to you, you will be filled with anger, frustration, and despair. To fight against God's right to say no to you is really the same thing as fighting against God. That's a battle you'll never win.

How much wiser it is to say, "Lord, I am praying this prayer from the bottom of my heart, but even as I pray I confess that You have the right to say no if that's what You think is best." You'll sleep well at night when you learn to pray like that.

And in this we have the example of the Lord Jesus who, when He prayed in the Garden of Gethsemane with the sweat pouring off Him like great drops of blood, said, "O my Father, if it be possible, let this cup pass from me: nevertheless not as I will, but as thou wilt" (Matthew 26:39 KJV). If Jesus needed to pray that way, how much more do we?

Let God be God in your life. Give Him the right to say no.

3. Keep on doing what you know to be right.

In the darkness of unanswered prayer, you may be tempted to give up on God. You may feel like throwing in the towel and checking out of the Christian life. But what good will that do? If you turn away from God, where will you go?

Keep on praying, keep on believing, keep on reading the Bible, keep on obeying, keep on following the Lord. If you stay on course in the darkness, eventually the light will shine again and you will be glad that you did not turn away in the moment of disappointment.

Until that morning comes and the sunlight of God's presence fills our faces, we move on through the twilight, knowing that some of our prayers will not be answered no matter how hard we pray. But this fact sustains us on our long journey home: He did not say, "My answers are sufficient," but rather, "My grace is sufficient for you."

4

CAN WE STILL BELIEVE IN ROMANS 8:28?

D o all things really work together for good? Consider the following.

- A little baby is born with no brain, only a brain stem. The doctors tell the parents that she has no chance of surviving. Somehow she stays alive for sixteen months. The parents struggle to take care of her. When she gets sick, the doctors tell the parents, "Don't bring her to the hospital. There is nothing we can do for her."

- A young lad of twelve goes with his church youth group on a Saturday outing. That night he comes down with a fever. The next morning he has trouble breathing and his mother calls the doctor. By the time the ambulance gets there, he has stopped breathing. The doctor does everything he can, but the boy is dead on arrival. He died from a strange bacterial infection.

- A man feels the call of God to go into the ministry. He leaves his good job and moves to a distant city to enter seminary. His wife takes a job to help him make it through. He's in his last year now. In just a few months he'll take a church somewhere and begin serving the Lord. But one day his wife comes in and says, "I'm leaving you. I don't want to be a pastor's wife." She walks out and never comes back.

- Another man is a policeman. One day he stops a man known to be a drug dealer. It happens on a busy downtown street and a crowd gathers to watch the unfolding drama. There is a struggle and somehow the drug dealer grabs the officer's gun. Someone in the crowd yells, "Shoot him, man." And he does, at point-blank range, in the face. The officer was in his early twenties.

Do all things work together for good? Do they? Can we still believe in Romans 8:28?

Let us be honest and admit that we have at least two problems with these words by the apostle Paul.

1. *They promise something we can't believe.* Our text says, "And we know that all things work together for good" (KJV). Paul, how can you be so sure about that? In truth, most of us are not as sure as Paul was. We hope all things work together for good; we believe they do. But do we really know that to be true?

2. *They include things that ought to be left out.* Paul says, "And we know that all things work together for good." All things? Does that include even the darkest tragedies of life? Sure, we know that some things work together for good. We understand that out of difficulty can come great lessons of faith that we cannot learn any other way. Yes, some things clearly work together for good. But can we be sure it is really all things? Perhaps these words are true in the theoretical sense or perhaps as a statement of faith. But they do not square with life as we know it.

I do not have to tell you that Romans 8:28 is one of the most beloved verses in the Bible. You know that. Many of you could give testimony to that fact. You were sick, and this verse was like medicine to your soul. You lost a loved one, and these words somehow carried you through. You were crushed and beaten by the winds of ill-fortune, and this verse—and only this verse!—gave you hope to go on.

Therefore, it shocks us to know that there are many who secretly doubt it. They hear this verse quoted, and instead of a balm to the soul, it is a mocking, cruel joke.

They say, "What do you mean by good?"

— Sickness is not good.
— Murder is not good.
— Divorce is not good.
— Rape is not good.
— The death of a child is not good.

This verse is sometimes misused. Well-meaning Christians sometimes throw it in the face of those who are suffering as if it could answer every question of life. When it is misused that way, it produces an effect opposite to that intended by Paul.

But like it or not, it's in the Bible. And it won't go away. Which brings us back to the basic question: Can we still believe in Romans 8:28?

Four considerations will help us answer that question. These are four perspectives we need to keep in mind as we read this verse. They are not original with me. During my doctoral studies, I attended a seminar taught by Dr. Vernon Grounds, the longtime president of Denver Seminary. One afternoon he shared these insights with us, and I am simply passing them along in this chapter.

THE TEXT NEEDS RETRANSLATING

Let's look at the first phrase in three different versions:

King James Version: "All things work together for good to them that love God."

New American Standard Bible: "God causes all things to work together for good."

New International Version: "In all things God works for the good of those who love him."

Did you catch the difference? In the King James version God is way down at the end of the phrase. In the other two versions God is at the beginning. It is partly a question of text and partly a question of grammar. There is nothing wrong with the traditional version, but the modern translations bring out a proper emphasis.

We will never properly understand this verse as long as we put God at the end and not at the beginning. But some people look at life that way. They believe that life is like a roll of the dice—sometimes you win and sometimes you lose. And they believe that after a tragedy, God shows up to make everything come out right. But that is not the biblical view at all.

In reality, *God is there at the beginning, and He is there at the end, and He is there at every point in between.* God is at work. Not luck, or chance, or blind fate. And that answers the great question, "Where is God when it hurts? Is He there at the beginning, or is He there only at the end?" The answer is that Romans 8:28 *begins* with God. He was there before it all happened, He is there when it happens, and He is still there after it is all over.

That forever puts an end to the happy-ever-afterism that says, "No matter what happens, God will turn a tragedy into a blessing." That's fine for fairy tales, but not for real life.

What do you say when a little child dies? Or when a cop is killed by a drug dealer? Or when a man dies on the mission field? Or when a woman is cheated out of her inheritance? Or when a friend dies of AIDS? Or when your marriage falls apart after thirty-eight years? It is hard to see how these are good.

When we look at these situations we must at all costs resist the cheap explanation. It's too quick, too easy. Sometimes tragedies happen and well-meaning people say, "That's not a tragedy. It only looks that way. Just have faith." If you believe that tragedy is not really tragedy, you will probably lose your faith altogether.

Suppose I have an accident and wreck my car. And suppose when I take it into the body shop, the man says, "Friend, you haven't had an accident. Your car has just been rearranged." And I turn and look at the cracked grille, the crumpled fender, the twisted bumper, and the shattered windshield. Then I say, "Buddy, you're crazy. This car isn't rearranged. It's wrecked."

The Bible never asks us to pretend that tragedy isn't tragedy or to pretend that our pain isn't real.

The point is, we must see the active involvement of God. What happens to you and to me is not the mechanical turning of some impersonal wheel. It is not fate or kismet or karma or luck. God is actively at work in your life!

Is Paul saying, "Whatever happens is good"? No.

Is he saying that suffering and evil and tragedy are good? No.

Is he saying everything will work out if we just have enough faith? No.

Is he saying that we will understand why God allowed tragedy to come? No.

What, then, *is* he saying? He is erecting a sign over the

unexplainable mysteries of life, a sign that reads, "Quiet. God at work." How? We're not always sure. To what end? Good, and not evil. That's what Romans 8:28 is saying.

Little children will often be afraid at night. They are scared because they can't see in the darkness. They cry out until at last Daddy comes. He sits on the bed and takes them in his arms and holds them and says, "Don't be afraid. I'm right here with you." The fear goes away when Daddy comes.

Even so, the darkness of life frightens us until we discover that our heavenly Father is there. The darkness is still dark, but He is there, and that makes all the difference.

Can we still believe in Romans 8:28? Yes, but we need to retranslate the text to bring God in at the beginning of the verse.

WE NEED A LONG-TERM PERSPECTIVE

So many things in life seem unexplainable. Why does a tornado destroy one house and leave another untouched? Why does one brother excel while another struggles all his life? Why does a tumor come back when the doctor said he thought he got it all? The list of such questions is endless. Seen in isolation, they make no sense whatsoever. If there is a purpose behind such tragedy, we cannot see it.

Our danger is that we will judge the end by the beginning. Or, to be more exact, that we will judge what we cannot see by what we can see. When tragedy strikes, if we can't see a purpose, we assume there isn't one.

But the very opposite is true. *We ought to judge the beginning by the end.* Here is where Romans 8:28 gives us some real help. Paul says, "And we know that all things *work together* for good." The phrase *work together* is really one word—*sunergon*—in Greek. We get our English word *synergy* from it. And what is synergy? It is what happens when you put two or more elements together to form something brand new that neither could form separately. It's what happens when my wife goes into the kitchen and makes a big pot of John Madden's Super Bowl Stew. She puts in the potatoes, the carrots, the celery, the rutabagas, the turnips, the spices, the meat, and a few other secret ingredients I know nothing about. What comes out is the best stew I've ever had. Now left to myself I would never eat rutabagas or turnips. But in the Super Bowl Stew they combine with all those other ingredients to produce a gastronomic delight. That's synergy—the combination of many elements to produce a positive result.

That's what Paul means when he says that God causes all things to "work together." Many of the things that make no sense when seen in isolation are in fact working together to produce something good in my life. There is a divine synergy even in the darkest moments, a synergy that produces something positive. And the "good" that is ultimately produced could not happen any other way.

Suppose you visit one of the mammoth automobile factories in Detroit. What you see there is an enormous building that covers many acres. At one end they bring in the raw materials and various component parts of an automobile—the engine, the wheels, the chassis, the frame, the outer body, the windshield, the instrument panel, the seats, the carpeting, and so on. Some of the parts you recognize; others are unfamiliar. But all of it is constantly being unloaded and brought inside. At the other end of the building—a vast distance away—a new car rolls out. From the outside, you see only one end and a dim glimpse of the other.

What happens in between? From the outside you cannot tell. You hear the noise from within, but you cannot see the process. But you know this much: That new car did not happen by chance. Inside the building intelligent minds and capable hands take the raw material and the component parts and from them fashion a car. What by itself seemed to have no purpose is in the end indispensable.

Paul is saying that our experience is like that. God

begins with the raw materials of life, including some parts that seem to serve no good purpose. Those materials are acted upon by pressure and heat and then are bent and shaped and joined together. Over time something beautiful is created. Not by accident, but by a divine design. And nothing is ever wasted in the process.

That is how we must look at life. We must not judge the end by the beginning, but rather the beginning by the end.

Can we still believe in Romans 8:28? Yes, we can. But we need a long-term perspective.

WE MUST DEFINE THE WORD "GOOD"

This is the crux of the matter. Paul says that "all things work together for good." But what is the "good" he is talking about? For most of us, "good" equals things like health, happiness, solid relationships, long life, money, food on the table, meaningful work, and a nice place to live. In general, we think the "good" life means a better set of circumstances.

Once again, that's not necessarily the biblical viewpoint. In this case we don't have to wonder what Paul means. He defines it for us in the very next verse: "For those God foreknew he also predestined to be conformed to the likeness of his Son" (8:29). That makes it very clear. God has predestined you and me to a certain end. That certain end is the "good" of Romans 8:28. It is that we might be conformed to the likeness of Jesus Christ.

Let me put it plainly. *God is at work in your life making you like Jesus Christ.* He has predestined you to that end. He is at work in your life making that happen. Therefore, anything that makes you more like Jesus Christ is good. Anything that pulls you away from Jesus Christ is bad.

When Paul says that all things work together for good, he is not saying that the tragedies and heartaches of life will always produce a better set of circumstances. Sometimes they do, sometimes they don't. But God is not committed to

66

making you happy and successful. He *is* committed to making you like His Son, the Lord Jesus Christ. And whatever it takes to make you more like Jesus is good.

So it is in the providence of God that we learn more in the darkness than we do in the light. We gain more from sickness than we do from health. We pray more when we are scared than when we are confident. And everything that happens to you—the tragedies, the unexplained circumstances, even the stupid choices you make—all of it is grist for the mill of God's loving purpose. He will not give up even when we do.

> I walked a mile with Pleasure,
> She chattered all the way.
> But I was none the wiser,
> For all she had to say.
> Then I walked a mile with Sorrow,
> And ne'er a word said she.
> But, oh, the lessons I did learn
> When Sorrow walked with me.
> Unknown

God is at work in your life. Right now, you are rough and uncut, and God is patiently chipping away at you. But remember this: He will never intentionally hurt you. In the end, you will look like the Lord Jesus Christ.

This, I think, is our greatest problem with Romans 8:28. Our good and God's good are not the same. We want happiness and fulfillment and peace and long life. Meanwhile, God is at work in us and through us and by everything that happens to us to transform us into the image of His Son.

Does that include the worst that happens to us? Yes.

Does that include the things that hurt us deeply? Yes.

Does that include the times when we are heartbroken? Yes.

Does that include the times when we sin? Yes.

Does that include the times when we doubt God? Yes.

Does that include the times when we curse Him to His face? Yes.

He is always at work. He is never deterred by us. Nothing happens to us outside His control. There are no mistakes and no surprises.

God can do that even when we can't.

God does it even when we don't believe it.

That is what Paul means when he says, "We know." We know it because we know God, and He has said it. His word is trustworthy, and that guarantees it. Indeed, His character rests upon it.

We know it not by looking at the events of life, but by knowing God. We know it not by studying the pattern of the cloth, but by knowing the designer of the fabric. We know it not by listening to the notes of the symphony, but by knowing the composer of the music.

There are many things we don't know. We don't know why babies die or why cars wreck or why planes crash or why families break up or why good people get sick and suddenly die. But this we do know—God is at work, and He has not forgotten us.

Can we still believe in Romans 8:28? Yes, but we must properly define what "good" means.

WE MUST UNDERSTAND THE LIMITATION OF THIS VERSE

Notice the last phrase of Romans 8:28. It is a promise to "those who love [God], who have been called according to his purpose." That is an all-important limitation. This verse is true of Christians and only of Christians. It is not a blanket promise to the whole human race. Why? Because God's purpose is to make His children one day like His Son.

Before he died of liver cancer, baseball star Mickey Mantle openly admitted that he had abused his body through years of hard living and hard drinking. At his funeral service Bobby Richardson gave the most important message when he told a packed sanctuary at the Lovers' Lane Methodist Church in Dallas how Mickey had called him and asked for prayer two days before he died. When he went to see him in the hospital that same day, Mickey brought the subject up. "I want you to know that I've accepted Jesus Christ as my Savior." Bobby Richardson wanted to make sure, so he shared the gospel anyway and explained what it meant to trust Christ as Savior. When he finished, Mickey Mantle said, "That's exactly what I did."

Bobby Richardson and his wife went back to visit Mickey Mantle again the day before he died. Mrs. Richardson asked Mickey a pointed question: "If you were to stand before God and He said to you, 'Why should I let you into my heaven?' what would you say?" He immediately replied, "For God so loved the world that he gave his only begotten Son that whosoever believeth in him should not perish but have everlasting life."

The next day, knowing that his death was near, he said with a smile on his face, "I'm ready to go now. Let's get on with it." He died within a few hours.

In spite of his fame and fortune, at the end his hands were empty. All those home runs and all those amazing catches and even that wonderful Oklahoma smile couldn't forgive even one of his sins. And by his own admission, he came to the end of his life with many sins that needed forgiveness.

Did Mickey Mantle go to heaven? I believe the answer is yes. He reached out with the empty hands of faith and took hold of Jesus Christ. The blood of Jesus Christ cleansed him from all his sins.

Dying of cancer is not "good" in the usual sense of the word. But cancer is "good" in the ultimate sense if it forces us to admit our need and turn to Jesus Christ for salvation. It is better to die with cancer knowing Jesus Christ than to live without cancer and also without Jesus.

Two Important Qualifications

And so we come back to the basic question: Can we still believe in Romans 8:28?

It sounds good.

We want to believe it.

I say that we *can* believe in Romans 8:28 as long as we keep two things in mind.

1. We must not try to explain the unexplainable.

Sometimes in our zeal to protect God, we try to explain why bad things happen to good people. That's almost always a bad idea. We are like little children looking into the face of an infinitely wise Father. It is not possible that we should understand all He does. It is enough that we love Him and know that He is there.

Let us be honest and confess that it is right at this point that so much damage has been done. In the end, it is not this verse that has lost its credibility, but rather our feeble attempts to justify the mysterious ways of God. Better to say nothing than to speak of things we know nothing about.

2. We must understand that God's values and our values are not the same.

This is really like saying, "We must understand that we will often not understand at all." Let us be clear on this point. We are not called to praise God for evil, sin, and death. But we can praise God for the good He can work in the darkest days of life.

Romans 8:28 is not teaching us to call evil good or simply to smile through the tears and pretend everything is OK. But it *is* teaching us that no matter what happens to us—no matter how terrible, no matter how unfair—our God is there. He has not left us. His purposes are being worked out as much in the darkness as they are in the light.

"Where Was God When My Son Died?"

The story is told of a father whose son was killed in a terrible accident. He came to his pastor and in great anger said, "Where was God when my son died?" The pastor thought for a moment and said, "The same place He was when His Son died."

That's the final piece of the puzzle. He knows what we are going through for He, too, has been there. He watched His own Son die.

Therefore, we can say with the apostle Paul, "We know." Not because we see the answer, but because we know Him—and He knows what it is like to lose a Son. He knows, and we know Him.

Can we still believe in Romans 8:28? Let me answer that question with another. What is your alternative? If you don't believe in Romans 8:28, what do you believe in? Fate? Chance? The impersonal forces of nature?

Yes, we can—and must—believe in Romans 8:28. It is teaching us one great truth: *All things ultimately contribute to the ultimate good of those who love God.*

That does not answer every question. But it does answer the big question: Does God know what He is doing? Yes, He does . . . and we know Him—and that is enough.

5

THE SENSITIVITY
OF JESUS

Have you ever felt so exhausted that you couldn't go on? If so, ponder this little slice of life as told by Luke.

As Jesus was on his way, the crowds almost crushed him. And a woman was there who had been subject to bleeding for twelve years, but no one could heal her. She came up behind him and touched the edge of his cloak, and immediately her bleeding stopped.

"Who touched me?" Jesus asked.

When they all denied it, Peter said, "Master, the people are crowding and pressing against you."

But Jesus said, "Someone touched me; I know that power has gone out from me."

Then the woman, seeing that she could not go unnoticed, came trembling and fell at his feet. In the presence of all the people, she told why she had touched him and how she had been instantly healed. Then he said to her, "Daughter, your faith has healed you. Go in peace." (Luke 8:42–48)

This story captured the heart and soul and imagination

of the early church. Over the generations a large tradition arose around this story, including the name of the woman who touched the hem of Jesus' garment. In the Greek church her name was Bernice; in the Coptic and Latin church it was Veronica. Eusebius says that she was a Gentile from Caesarea Philippi and that when she returned home after her healing, she erected a statue of Jesus in her front yard. All these things amount to interesting speculation, but none of them are verifiable. They do, however, point out the hold this story had on the first-century church.

What we really have here is a miracle within a miracle. In all three accounts in the Bible of the incident (Matthew 9, Mark 5, Luke 8), this miracle takes place within the context of the raising of Jairus's daughter. It happened like this. One day as Jesus was teaching in one of the villages along the shore of the Sea of Galilee, a man named Jairus came and begged Jesus to come to his house and heal his twelve-year-old daughter, who was desperately sick. As Jesus began to walk with Jairus toward his house, hundreds of people began to press in upon Him, many of them no doubt hoping for their own cure, many others listening to His every word, still others attracted by all the commotion.

If you have ever been to the Holy Land, you know how narrow and crowded the streets are. In some places you can almost reach out and touch the buildings on both sides of the street. So we know the scene must have been chaotic and confusing—Jairus on one side of Jesus tugging at His sleeve ("Hurry, Lord, my daughter is dying"); the disciples forming a moving wave like bodyguards for a celebrity; hundreds of eager people pushing, milling, shouting, stretching out their arms to touch Him as He passes by. Meanwhile, totally unnoticed, a frail, stooped, sickly woman pushes her way through the throng. Her face is partially covered so no one will recognize her. Her arms are thin; her hands shake as she stretches them toward Jesus. Now she is only a few feet away. Now He is passing right by her. No one notices as she reaches out to touch the blue and white tassel on the corner of His cloak.

AN ISSUE OF BLOOD

The Bible is not very specific about her problem, and the translators handle it in different ways. The King James Version says she had "an issue of blood" for twelve years. The modern translations speak of a hemorrhage of blood. Most commentators agree it was some kind of chronic uterine bleeding. Whether continual or periodic, it was not normal, and in those days, there was no cure for that condition.

But that wasn't the worst of it. Leviticus 15:25–27 contains certain regulations for women with an uncontrollable flow of blood. The passage says that such women are to be considered unclean and defiled as long as the flow of blood continues. Furthermore, anyone who touched such a woman would himself become unclean and defiled.

In a practical sense, this meant that this poor woman had become an outcast in her own village. G. Campbell Morgan describes her situation:

> By the law of Moses this woman was not allowed to touch any human being, and no human being was allowed to touch her. The law demanded that a woman suffering in this way should be segregated. . . . For twelve years this woman had been excommunicated from the Temple and from the synagogue, from every religious place of assembly. . . . [She was] divorced from her husband, shut out from her family, ostracized by society, and treated as a pariah.[1]

She had endured incurable illness, social isolation, constant pain, financial poverty, and personal humiliation. It is hard to imagine a more pitiful situation. In the words of one writer, she had been among the "living dead" for twelve long years. Now, at last, Jesus has come to her village.

DOCTOR, DOCTOR

In Mark's version of this story one detail is included that Luke omits. Mark 5:26 notes that this woman "had suffered a great deal under the care of many doctors and had spent all she had, yet instead of getting better she grew worse." Why do you think Luke left that detail out? Probably because he was a physician and he didn't want to make his own profession look bad.

Actually, that verse doesn't imply that the doctors back then were all quacks. What it means is that they simply didn't have any effective treatments for this kind of chronic hemorrhaging. As a matter of fact, the Talmud lists several "cures" for this problem: (1) drinking a goblet of wine containing a powder composed of rubber, alum, and garden crocuses; (2) eating Persian onions cooked in wine administered with the words "Arise out of your flow of blood"; (3) carrying the ash of an ostrich egg in a certain cloth. With "cures" like that, it's no wonder the woman wasn't getting any better.

It's also no surprise that she had been to many doctors and had spent all her money. The Mishnah (the Jewish oral commentary on the law) contains this frank opinion on doctors by one Rabbi Judah: "Ass-drivers are most of them wicked, camel-drivers are most of them proper folk, sailors are most of them saintly, but the best among physicians are destined for Hell."

The doctors simply could not help her. For twelve years she had suffered from this "issue of blood." Her prognosis was grim. Without a miracle, there was no hope.

TOUCHING THE TASSEL

Now Jesus has come to her village. The word spreads like wildfire. "He's here." "Who's here?" "Jesus, that man from Nazareth who heals the sick. He just came to town, and Jairus is talking to Him." With that, the poor woman makes the decision that somehow, someway she must get through to see Jesus. If only she could touch Him.

Perhaps there was a bit of superstition in her faith. Perhaps she thought there was some kind of "magic" in His clothing. Who knows? *If only I can reach out and touch the hem of His garment, perhaps that will be enough.* In truth, her faith was immature and incomplete. And yes, it was mixed with a kind of folk magic. But it was enough to make her risk public rejection and reach out with a sickly hand to the Son of God.

But there's something else at work here. She did not speak to Him because she was embarrassed and ashamed of her condition. After twelve years of public humiliation, she wouldn't risk exposure and the taunts of the crowd. She thought to simply touch Him, receive her healing, and then slip away unnoticed. After so many years, she was used to coping with life that way.

Now she reaches out and touches Jesus. The old versions speak of "the hem of his garment." That's certainly an acceptable translation, but the Greek word probably refers to one of the four tassels all Jewish men wore on their outer garments. Numbers 15:37–41 specified that tassels must be sewn on the four corners of the cloak and that each must contain a blue thread. The tassels were visual reminders to obey God's commandments. No matter the design of the cloak, at least one of the tassels would always hang from the back of the wearer. It was this tassel that the woman touched as Jesus walked by.

The text is very clear on what happened when she touched the tassel. Two different words are used. She was *immediately* (Luke 8:44) and *instantly* (v. 47) healed. The text even specifies that at the moment she touched the tassel, the bleeding stopped.

It was a vast miracle. Jesus is going the other direction, Jairus tugging at Him and talking and crying all at the same time. Meanwhile, the crowd is so tightly packed in the narrow alleyway that a person could hardly breathe, much less move. The disciples are trying to do crowd control, but they are swept along with the flow. No one sees this wretched woman off to the side, no one notices as she elbows her way to the center, no one pays attention as she reaches out her hand, no one speaks to her and she speaks to no one.

Here comes Jesus! Even He does not notice this woman. As He passes by, her hand brushes His tassel. Something like an electrical shock moves from her fingers through her hand, up her arm, and into every part of her body. Only it is not an electrical shock, but the infusion of some mighty power with which she was not familiar. And in less time than it takes to tell it, her weary arteries, shrunken veins, diseased organs, withered muscles, and shattered nerves are filled with health and life and strength. The disastrous decay of twelve years is instantly halted and then reversed.

She is well again! Healthy again! Whole again!

She turns to go, not ungrateful—no, not at all—but fearful lest she call attention to herself and respectful of the greater work Jesus must do. She must not bother Him. With a smile on her face, the first real smile in a long, long time, she turns to go home.

"Who Touched Me?"

But just at that moment, Jesus stops, turns, and surveying the crowd asks, "Who touched Me?" It seems to Peter and the other disciples like an absurd question. Hundreds of people were milling around and He wants to know who touched Him? Everybody was touching Him. So many people were crowding around Jesus it could have been anyone. Besides, what difference does it make? A touch is a touch is a touch.

But that's not true. In the gospels there are three kinds of touches. First, there is the touch of *hostility*. That's the touch of the religious leaders when they beat Jesus at His trial. Second, there is the touch of *curiosity*. That's the touch of the crowd milling around. Third, there is the touch of *faith*. That's the touch of this poor woman. If the disciples couldn't tell the difference, no matter, Jesus could. He knew that someone had touched Him in faith. He felt the faith in the passing brush of her fingers on His tassel.

Please note that He did not ask the question for His own benefit. He knew before He turned who had touched Him. He's the Son of God, after all. He asked not for His sake, but for her sake and for the sake of the crowd.

He asked for her sake so that He could raise the level of her faith. If she went away without a further word, she might actually believe there was some magic power in His clothing. He wanted to assure her that it was her faith in *Him* that made the difference. Furthermore, He wanted her to know that the healing would be permanent. Finally, He wanted to establish a personal relationship with her. For all those things to be accomplished, she needed to identify herself to Jesus and to the crowd.

He also asked "Who touched Me?" for the sake of the crowd. So that Jairus would know what Jesus could do. So that the curious onlookers would see His power fully displayed. And perhaps most important, He wanted the crowd to know that He wasn't ashamed to be touched by the untouchable.

This woman had taken a real chance by touching Jesus. According to the law, her touch could make Jesus unclean. But because He was the Son of God, His power of healing overcame her uncleanness. But she did not know that when she touched Him.

What a crucial point this is. Our Lord Jesus was not ashamed to be touched by the untouchable, and He was not embarrassed to be publicly identified with the outcasts of this world. He was at home with publicans and sinners, He ate supper with gluttons and drunkards, He welcomed the prostitutes, He touched the lepers and, in this story, He is not ashamed to be touched by an unclean person.

Not ashamed? No, not at all. Delighted, I think, and glad to identify Himself with her. Delighted that she had the courage to reach out and glad that He could heal her. And He didn't care who knew about it. No, that's not strong enough. He *wanted* the whole crowd to know what He had done.

Why is this so important? Because with our Lord there are no "untouchable" people. In Jesus' eyes, everyone is touchable. Thank God, there are no hopeless cases with Him.

"POWER HAS GONE OUT OF ME"

"Someone touched me; I know that power has gone out from me" (v. 46). These strange words mean at least this much: that Jesus was conscious of God's power flowing out from Him into the body of the woman who touched His garment. Power that had been His passed from Him to her. It resulted in her healing, but the power had to go out from Him first.

There is a universal truth here. If you follow Jesus and get involved with the needy people of this world, you will be conscious of power flowing out from your life as well. By definition those in need lack the strength necessary to face the challenges of life. The only way they can get strength or power is from those who have more than they do. Ministering to such people means that power or strength or virtue will flow out from your life to theirs. It will cost you something that you will not easily replace—the very strength of your own life.

Many years ago T. DeWitt Talmage said it this way: "There is no addition of help to others, without the subtraction of power from ourselves." Then he elaborated:

> Now if omnipotence cannot help others without depletion, how can we ever expect to bless the world without self-sacrifice? A man who gives to some Christian object until he feels it, a man who in his occupation or profession overworks that he may educate his children, a man who on Sunday night

goes home, all his nervous energy wrung out by active service in Church, or Sabbath-school, or city evangelization, has imitated Christ, and the strength has gone out of him. A mother who robs herself of sleep in behalf of a sick child, a wife who bears up cheerfully under domestic misfortune that she may encourage her husband in the combat against disaster, a woman who by hard saving, and earnest prayer, and good counsel, wisely given, and many years devoted to rearing her family for God and usefulness and heaven, and who has nothing to show for it but premature gray hairs, and a profusion of deep wrinkles, is like Christ, and strength has gone out of her.[2]

This truth explains something that many people have puzzled over. When Jesus was finally crucified, why did He die so quickly? The Romans assumed that when they crucified someone it would take twenty-four to forty-eight hours for that person to die. But Jesus died after only six hours on the cross. Why? Was it not because He had spent His life giving Himself for others, and when He finally came to the end, He had given and given and given, and from a human point of view, He had given all that He had? May that not be at least part of the explanation? Sometimes we say (in a sentimental way), "He died of a broken heart." There is at least this much truth in that statement: When He died, He was exhausted from giving Himself for others.

If you follow Jesus, the same thing will happen to you. You will give and give and the power will go out from you. You can help people, but it will cost you something. Not just time, not just energy, not just money, but your very life. Strength will go out from you into the lives of the people you help. They will grow stronger; you will grow weaker. In the end, like Jesus, you too will be exhausted. You may not live as long as you would like. But when you die, you will have the satisfaction of knowing that you lived your life for others and that the strength that has gone out from you has not been wasted on the trivial pursuits of this world.

"GO IN PEACE"

Our story is almost ended. When Jesus asks, "Who touched me?" the woman knows He is talking about her. Luke says that she came trembling and fell at Jesus' feet. Then she publicly declared what Jesus had done for her and how she had been instantly healed. I imagine there was clapping and cheering all around and Jairus saying, "That's good. Now come on, Jesus, my little girl needs you."

But before they go on, Jesus looks at the woman and says, "Daughter, your faith has healed you" (v. 48). The word for *daughter* is unusual. It's the only time the gospels record Jesus using this particular word. It's a term of affectionate endearment, something like "Maiden," or "Little girl," or even "Sweetheart." Then He said, "Go in peace," or literally, "Go *into* peace," meaning "Go from this place and walk in good health. You are healed forever of your disease."

TWO ENDURING PICTURES

Before we wrap up this chapter, let us focus on two enduring pictures that remain from this story. They are images of Jesus and of this woman that encourage us along the way.

The Sensitivity of Jesus

A few days ago I heard on the radio that *Playboy* magazine has said that the ideal man of the nineties is the sensitive, caring man who isn't afraid to show his feelings. They also said that the selfish bachelor of the eighties is out.

But I'll tell you something that *Playboy* magazine doesn't know and wouldn't find out in a thousand years. *The most sensitive man in all history is Jesus Christ.* No one ever cared about people like He did. No one ever gave of Himself like He did. No one ever felt the pain of others like He did.

He is—and was, and always will be—the most truly sensitive man to ever walk the face of the earth.

As He walked down a crowded street, hundreds of hands reached out to Him. Yet He felt the thin, sickly hand of faith. He felt it! He felt her touch . . . He stopped . . . He turned . . . He spoke to her.

He was not offended or angry with her. Nor was He too busy or too tired to bother with her. Think of it. He whom all the forces of hell could not stop was diverted by the touch of a sickly hand! This woman did by her touch what Satan himself could not do. She stopped Jesus in His tracks.

And He spoke to her as if she were the only person in the crowd. When He turned, it was just Jesus and her. No one else mattered.

He loves you as if there were only one person in all the universe to love. He hears you as if you were the only one speaking to Him. He attends to your needs as if yours were the only needs in all the universe. What a Christ!

All that touches you touches Him. If it is pain, then He feels the pain. If it is sorrow, then He feels the sorrow. If it is rejection, then He feels the rejection. If it is loss, then He feels the loss. If it is failure, then He feels the failure. Whatever it is that hurts you, He feels it. If it touches you, it touches Him.

That's what the writer to the Hebrews meant when he said, "For we do not have a high priest who is unable to sympathize with our weaknesses" (Hebrews 4:15). Thank God it is so. If it hurts us, it hurts Him.

We do not have a stoic, uncaring Christ. Nor do we have a preoccupied Christ who is too busy to notice our problems, or an unemotional Christ who runs the universe like some high-powered businessman. He is the sensitive Jesus who, as the hymn writer says, "feels our deepest woe."

The Power of Feeble Faith

This story reveals to us a second picture. In this poor woman we see the amazing power of feeble faith. She didn't have a huge amount of faith, and what she had was partially misdirected. But she had a mustard seed, and through it God moved the mountain of her illness.

This story means that we don't have to agonize over the "correct" way to come to God. You don't have to worry about crossing all your "t's" or dotting all your "i's." You don't have to know the Bible before you come to God and you don't have to have a degree in theology. You don't even have to be a member of a church. Those things are good, but they aren't the main thing. If you come to Jesus Christ in simple faith—even though your faith be as feeble as this woman's was—He will not turn you away.

Do you ever feel as if your problems keep you from coming to God? Do you ever feel so dirty and unclean that you think Jesus would not have anything to do with you? Do not despair. Jesus is not offended by your problems. He's seen it all before. I say it again. He will not turn you away.

How simple it is to come to Christ! Only a touch, and this woman is healed. Not by her toiling, not by her promises to do better, not by an offer to do something for Jesus if He would do something for her. No deals here. She reached out a trembling hand and in an instant she was healed. It was not a long process. It happened so fast that it could only be called a miracle.

That's what feeble faith can do. Coming to Christ is not difficult. The hardest part is reaching out with the hand of faith. If you want to touch Jesus, all you have to do is reach out to Him.

"CAN I BE A CHRISTIAN?"

Several years ago I received an unusual letter from an international student who had been attending the church I pastor. This is what she said:

> Dear Dr. Ray Pritchard,
>   I have come to your church about two months, and I like [it] there a lot. I began to read the Bible by myself, and I want to be a Christian. However, I don't know how I can be a Christian. I want to talk to you about it, but I am a little shy, so I write to you. Can I be a Christian? Would you tell me how I am able to be a Christian?
>   I am looking forward to hearing from you. Thank you very much.
>   (I'm sorry, my writing is not too good.)

How do you answer a letter like that? Even though she is just learning English, you can sense the deep desire of her heart coming through those simple words.

This is part of my reply to her:

> You asked, "Can I be a Christian?" The answer is yes. You can be a Christian. The most important thing I can say to you is that being a Christian means having a personal relationship with Jesus Christ.
>   How do you get to know Jesus Christ personally? There must be a desire in your heart, which there already is. And you are already reading the Bible, which is God's message to you about Jesus Christ. So the good news is that you are not far from being a Christian right now!
>   In order to have a personal relationship with Jesus Christ, you must trust Him as your Savior. Does that sound strange? I hope not. Already you know much about Jesus. You know that He worked many miracles and helped many people. But the most important thing to know about Jesus is that He died on the cross for your sins. That is, when He died on the cross 2,000 years ago, He took your place. You should have died there. But He died in your place, as your substitute, and by His death He paid the price for all your sins.

That's a lot to think about, and you don't have to fully understand it (no one fully understands it), but you do have to believe it. That's what trusting is. It's believing, really believing in your heart that something is true. Trusting is what you do when you get on an airplane. You trust your life to the fact that the airplane will safely take you up in the air and then safely get you back to the ground again. That's trust. It's staking your life upon something you believe to be true.

Trusting Jesus Christ means staking your life upon the fact that when He died on the cross, He really did pay the price for your sins and He really did take your place.

So, do you believe that Jesus Christ died for you? Are you willing to stake your life upon that fact? If you are ready to say yes, then you can be a Christian.

Let me give you a simple prayer to pray. This prayer is not magic. You should only pray it if it expresses the real feeling of your heart. But if it does, then you can pray this prayer:

> Dear Lord, Jesus,
>
> Thank you for dying on the cross for me. Thank you for taking all my sin away. I believe You are the Son of God and the Savior of the world. I gladly take You as my Savior. Come into my life and make me a Christian. Please help me to live a life that will be pleasing to You. Thank You for hearing this prayer. Amen.

That's simple, isn't it? If you will pray that prayer and mean it from your heart, you can become a Christian right now. I hope you will just stop right now and pray that prayer to God.

Did you pray that prayer? I hope so. If you did, I would be honored if you would tell me so. On Sunday, if you do not feel too shy about it, you can just come up to me and say, "Pastor Ray, I prayed that prayer." I would be so happy if you would do that.

I put that letter in the mail and wondered how my friend would receive it. Would it make sense? Would she understand it?

The very next Sunday she came up to me after the worship service and said with a shy smile that she had gotten my letter. I asked her if she had read it. She said yes. I asked her if she had prayed the prayer. She said yes. I asked if she understood what the prayer meant. She said yes. I asked if the prayer expressed the desire of her heart. She said yes.

Then I said, "Welcome. You are now a Christian." She said, "That's all I have to do be a Christian?" When I said yes, the most beautiful smile I have ever seen spread across her face from one side to the other.

REACH OUT AND TOUCH HIM

That's the power of feeble faith when it is directed toward the right object. You don't have to have strong faith. You can have weak faith so long as it is resting upon a strong object. And who could be stronger than Jesus Christ Himself?

How simple it is to come to Christ! Just a touch, that's all it takes. If you have the strength to stretch out your hand to Him, His mighty power will flow into your life.

NOTES

1. G. Campbell Morgan, *The Gospel According to Luke* (New York: Revell, 1931), 115.
2. T. DeWitt Talmage, *Treasury of T. DeWitt Talmage*, ed. May Talmage (Grand Rapids: Baker, 1968) 142–43.

6

WHY GOD MAKES IT HARD WHEN IT OUGHT TO BE EASY

Sometimes you find the best truth in the strangest places.

One of the great proofs of the Bible's supernatural origin is that it speaks to every part of the human condition. Not only is there something for everyone in the Bible, but there is something meaningful for every situation we face in life.

We would expect nothing less from a book that claims to be the very Word of God. If the message of the Bible comes directly from God, then it ought to speak to us at the precise point of our spiritual need.

In the preceding chapters we have explored some crucial questions about the character of God and human suffering. Now we want to step back and look at a new question: Why does God make it hard when it ought to be easy?

In order to answer that question, let's take a safari to an often-overlooked portion of the Bible—2 Samuel 2–3. These chapters tell the story of David's long struggle to become king over all Israel.

There are two facts that will help you understand this story. The first is that during this period Saul was dead and had been dead for some time. The second is that David had been anointed king over Judah and was living in the Levitical city of Hebron. Everything that happens in this story flows from those two facts.

The fact that Saul was dead meant that the throne of Israel was now vacant. Saul had forfeited his right to that throne through disobedience and rebellion. He had died in disgrace, committing suicide on the slopes of Mount Gilboa in a battle with the Philistines. Some of his supporters had rescued his body and given it a decent burial in Jabesh. And that brings up the point that Saul *did* have his followers. Lots of them, in fact. After all, he was the only king Israel had ever known, and even though he came to a bad end, there were thousands who mourned his death. But for good or ill, Saul was dead, the throne was vacant, and, since nature abhors a vacuum, something was bound to happen.

The fact that David was king in Judah meant that he was still marking time in Hebron. He was God's choice to rule the nation after the death of Saul. And you would think, from a purely human point of view, that this was his big chance. At the age of thirty, David seemed fully prepared to take over. But it didn't work that way. Nothing in life is ever that easy.

DAVID'S RISING STAR

In order to understand these two chapters, there are five people you need to keep straight in your mind. I'm going to list them in two columns to make it simple.

	~~SAUL~~
DAVID	**ISH-BOSHETH**
JOAB	**ABNER**

David, of course, was the king in Judah. There is a line through Saul in the chart because he was dead. Ish-Bosheth was one of Saul's surviving sons. He became a puppet king in Saul's place. Joab was David's number one general and Abner was Saul's number two general.

What it all meant was that after Saul's death the nation was divided along north-south lines. The people in the north followed Ish-Bosheth and Abner. The people in the south followed David and Joab. Thus the stage was set for a civil war. Second Samuel 3:1 puts it this way: "The war between the house of Saul and the house of David lasted a long time."

As I read this passage, one question comes to mind: *Why did David have to fight for what God had already promised him?* To put it in modern terms, why couldn't David just "name it and claim it"? Why this civil war if David was really God's man to be king? Was there sin in his life? Was he out of God's will? The answer to both questions is no. Then why didn't God do what He had promised without all this fighting?

It's Not As Easy As It Looks

It's a question everyone has struggled with at one time or another:

- A young couple moves from Indiana to Florida to go to seminary. From the moment they get here, things fall apart. They can't pay their bills, he can barely stay in school, she works full-time just to pay the bills, and the kids haven't had new clothes in over a year. They came because they felt God's call on their lives. *Why does God make it hard when it ought to be easy?*
- Another couple is married for almost twenty-five years when he suddenly, strangely comes down with a virus. The doctors treat it but he gets worse, not better. In two weeks he is dead. Life for her will never be the same. Deep in her heart, in the middle of a sleepless

night, she wonders, *Why does God make it hard when it ought to be easy?*

- He's six feet, two inches tall, one hundred-forty-two pounds dripping wet. He learned to run when he was in high school. Even when he spent two years working with a missionary in the arctic, he ran across the frozen tundra almost every day. His specialty was the 5,000-meter event. He made it to the Olympic trials and then tore his Achilles tendon. It was as close as he would get to the gold medal. You can't blame him for asking, *Why does God make it hard when it ought to be easy?*

- It started with forgetfulness that soon led to periods of incoherence. Eventually she could not take care of herself, so her husband hired a live-in housekeeper. Although she was only in her early sixties, the doctor confirmed the diagnosis: Alzheimer's disease. For over three years she was confined in a special unit of a nursing home. For months on end she sat motionless in a chair, her hands clenched, her legs permanently crossed. With tears her husband prayed over and over for her to be released from the ravages of an incurable disease. *Why does God make it hard when it ought to be easy?*

- A young church with a bright future calls a promising young pastor. After impressive early growth, the church splits and then falls apart. No one can understand it because there were so many good people with so much willing spirit. The future was almost unlimited. Now the pastor is gone and the church is a shadow of its former self. *Why does God make it hard when it ought to be easy?*

The story from David's life in 2 Samuel 2–3 provides a framework for answering that question. Why did David have to fight for what God had already promised him? These two chapters—which are basically about a civil war in Israel—suggest two answers.

1. That the rightness of his cause could be slowly revealed (2:11–3:5).

The key is the word *slowly.* David was thirty when he became king in Hebron. He was thirty-seven when he finally ruled the whole nation. What was God doing during that seven-year period? He was demonstrating to the people of Israel that David was indeed His man. We see this fact in two ways.

a. In the victories his soldiers won in battle (2:12–3:1).

"Abner son of Ner, together with the men of Ish-Bosheth son of Saul, left Mahanaim and went to Gibeon. Joab son of Zeruiah and David's men went out and met them at the pool of Gibeon. One group sat down on one side of the pool and one group on the other side." (They weren't getting ready to play chess. This is like the team captains meeting at the center of the field before a football game.)

"Then Abner said to Joab, 'Let's have some of the young men get up and fight hand to hand in front of us.'

"'All right, let them do it,' Joab said.

"So they stood up and were counted off—twelve men for Benjamin and Ish-Bosheth son of Saul, and twelve for David. Then each man grabbed his opponent by the head and thrust his dagger into his opponent's side, and they fell down together" (2 Samuel 2:12–16).

This is like one of those wrestling spectaculars where twelve men get in the ring at once. Only here it's twenty-four men, and they all end up killing each other. It's a tie. So they just go ahead and have a regular battle, and verse 17 says, "The battle that day was very fierce, and Abner and the men of Israel were defeated by David's men." If you want the body count, just drop down to verse 30: "Then Joab" (remember, he's on David's side) "returned from pursuing Abner and assembled all his men. Besides Asahel" (that's Joab's brother, who was killed by Abner) "nineteen of David's men were found missing. But David's men had killed three hundred and sixty Benjamites who were with Abner." That's like winning a football game 360 to 20. It's a kill ratio of 18 to 1 in David's favor. The whole point is that God was demonstrating that David was His man by giving him overwhelming victory on the battlefield.

b. In the birth of his six sons at Hebron (3:2–5).

Notice what the last part of 3:1 says. "David grew stronger and stronger, while the house of Saul grew weaker and weaker." We've already seen how that was true on the battlefield. But look what comes next. Verses 2–5 are a list of six sons who were born to David by six different women while he was in Hebron. The sons are Amnon, Kileab, Absalom, Adonijah, Shephatiah, and Ithream. Among the wives, the one we know best is Abigail, the widow of Nabal.

At first glance you may wonder why this list of sons is placed here. It appears to be out of place, but it isn't. In the ancient world one way a king demonstrated his power and greatness was by having many sons by many women. That's what this passage is stressing. That is, David was not only growing stronger on the battlefield, he was also growing stronger in the bedroom. That's hard for us to accept, but there it is.

But this is polygamy, you say. Yes, and it was never God's highest and best plan for mankind. But God permitted it in the Old Testament. David indulged himself this way, and he is still called "a man after God's heart." But—and this is a big but—one of the sons mentioned here is Absalom, who was to bring him nothing but heartache and shame.

Thus David was sowing the seeds that would later bring forth bitter fruit. For the moment, though, these sons were a sign of God's blessing.

And that's the first answer to the question, Why did David have to fight for what God had promised? Because in the fighting and in the waiting God was writing His will in the sky for all Israel to see. It was as plain as day. Only the blind could miss it. David was God's man—on the battlefield and in the bedroom.

2. That the purity of his motives might be openly revealed (3:6–39).

If the first reason had to do with external things, this one has to with David's heart. It was important that the people of Israel knew that David was not only God's man, but that he was the right kind of man. That is, they had to be convinced that God's choice ought to be their choice as well. God did that by arranging the circumstances so that the purity of David's motives might be openly revealed. This also happened in two ways.

a. In his willingness to welcome Abner to his side (3:6–21).

I've already mentioned that Abner was Saul's number one general. After Saul's death, he becomes the most powerful man in Israel. He is the one who put up Ish-Bosheth as a kind of puppet king. But make no mistake, Abner was the power behind the throne.

Second Samuel 3:6–21 tells us how Abner came over to David's side. It happened because Ish-Bosheth accused him of sleeping with Rizpah, one of Saul's concubines. In the ancient world, women were a symbol of political power, and the more women a man had, the more power he had. Thus a king might have many wives and many concubines, and all of them together would make up his harem. Rizpah was part of

Saul's harem. After he died, the harem more or less passed on to Ish-Bosheth.

When Ish-Bosheth accused Abner of sleeping with Rizpah, he was essentially accusing him of trying to pull a bedroom coup d'état. This is how Abner responded (v. 8): "Am I a dog's head—on Judah's side? This very day I am loyal to the house of your father Saul and to his family and friends. I haven't handed you over to David. Yet now you accuse me of an offense involving this woman!"

Abner was so upset that he decided to leave Ish-Bosheth and join David. It is here that you see something of David's heart. After some negotiation, he welcomed Abner into his camp. In fact, verse 20 says that David threw a feast for him and his men down in Hebron. It is a mark of his greatness that he would welcome a man who had recently been on the other side.

If you read the story of David's life, you will find that he had many character flaws. But one of his great strengths was that he knew how to forgive the past and turn enemies into friends. In welcoming Abner, David's heart was openly revealed for all to see.

b. In his grief at Abner's untimely death (3:22–39).

This was the final episode of the civil war. David had won on the battlefield and the opposing general had come over to his side. But before peace could be declared, Abner was assassinated.

It happened because Joab was jealous of Abner and did not trust him. Remember, they had just been fighting each other. And in that battle, Abner had been forced to kill Joab's brother Asahel in self-defense. So the assassination was partly revenge and partly jealousy.

Joab set up a trap to catch Abner alone at the well of Sirah. Verse 27 picks up the story. "Now when Abner returned to Hebron, Joab took him aside into the gateway, as though to speak with him privately. And there, to avenge the blood of his brother Asahel, Joab stabbed him in the stomach, and he died."

What would David do? If he sided with Joab, the people of Israel would think he set the whole thing up. If that happened, they would never trust him as king. His reaction was critical. It took place in five parts.

First, *he pronounced a curse on Joab and his house (vv. 28–29).*

Second, *he declared a period of public mourning (vv. 31–32).*

Third, *he composed a lament for Abner (vv. 33–34).*

Fourth, *he entered a personal fast (v. 35).*

Fifth, *he spoke of his personal anguish (vv. 38–39).*

Notice how the people responded to David's grief. "All the people took note and were pleased; indeed, everything the king did pleased them. So on that day all the people and all Israel knew that the king had no part in the murder of Abner son of Ner" (2 Samuel 3:36–37).

This may seem small to you, but I assure you it was big to the people of Israel. *The way a man responds in a time of crisis tells a great deal about his character.* In this case, David's grief revealed the purity of his motives. He was not trying to take the throne by devious means.

It's Not Easy to Wait for God

Let me summarize what we learn about David's life from this story. God had a purpose in making David fight for what He had promised. Through the years of struggle and controversy the rightness of his cause was slowly revealed. Through the events involving Abner, the purity of his motives was openly revealed. By the end of it all, two things were clear:

1. David was God's man to be king.
2. David was the right man to be king.

How does all this apply to us? I submit that David's life is a pattern of how God deals with His children. It helps us understand why God makes it hard when it ought to be easy. Why do seminary students struggle? Why do godly men get passed over for promotions? Why do some people reel from one catastrophe to another? Why do some women struggle for years to overcome the memories of their past? Why do some couples spend all their lives almost-but-not-quite making it? Why do so many people have to wait so long for something really good to happen in their lives? And, last, why do some churches seem to take three steps forward and two steps back?

The episodes in David's life we have just discussed demonstrate four steps God is taking when He makes it hard when it ought to be easy. It is God's plan to:

1. Vindicate us slowly.
2. Bless us openly.
3. Surprise us occasionally.
4. Test us continually.

Those four things taken together explain much of what happens to us. Some of you right now are in the vindication process. You are in the middle of a hard and difficult time, but it is God's intention to ultimately display the rightness of your cause. It's just not happening very fast. Some of you are being blessed openly, and that's a wonderful thing. Enjoy it, because it won't last forever. Some of you are being surprised by God with an unusual and unexpected circumstance. That is part of God's serendipity. And all of us are being tested continually. That, too, is part of God's plan.

THE LAWSUIT

I discovered this truth in a very personal way when I was named as a defendant in a lawsuit a few years ago. Although the particular details do not matter, it is important to know that the lawsuit arose after an attempt by our church to practice biblical church discipline. I was named in the lawsuit, along with another member of my staff and several lay volunteers. To make matters more complicated, several other churches and leaders were also named in the suit.

Up to that point I had never seriously considered the possibility that I might be sued in connection with my ministry. Although I spent four years in seminary, I don't remember hearing the subject raised in a single class. To be sure, I was aware of several high-profile cases around the country, and I knew that the incidence of such lawsuits had risen dramatically over the years, but I never once stopped to think that it might happen to me.

But it did, and for nearly five years I lived under the constant shadow of a jury trial. As far as I was concerned, we had acted cautiously and responsibly in light of the facts as we had known them. Looking back, I couldn't see any evidence that we had acted maliciously or recklessly.

You Never Know

But it wasn't my opinion that mattered. And the fact that we had biblical justification for taking action didn't matter in a court of law. I knew all too well that no one could predict in advance how a given jury might react to the evidence in the case. They might find me and my church guilty in spite of our good intentions and biblical convictions. For that matter, the fact that our church was well-known for taking a strong stand for the Bible might actually be used against us. Stranger things have happened.

Part of the problem revolved around trying to explain to a jury what church discipline is all about. By definition, any randomly chosen jury will contain people from many different religious backgrounds, and some with no religious background whatsoever. How do you explain Matthew 18 in that setting?

For three years the case bounced around the legal system. Twice it went to the Illinois Supreme Court on various motions—and twice we won. For months at a time we would hear nothing, then suddenly there would be a flurry of activity. Letters came from our lawyers advising us of motions, counter-motions, interrogatories, requests for more discovery, and so on. When the case went to the state supreme court for the third time, the justices ruled that there was an issue of fact that must be decided in a jury trial.

I think the worst moment for me personally came when we received a letter from our church insurance company informing us that if we were found guilty of a certain charge, they were reserving their right not to cover us for any potential damages. In plain English that meant if we were found guilty, our insurance might not pay the damages assessed against us. That might mean losing my life savings and even the house we had just purchased.

Living with the "What Ifs"

After three years, the opposing attorneys finally conducted a deposition. Although I had been briefed in advance, it was a harrowing experience to be questioned in minute detail about events that had occurred years earlier. If I expressed the slightest hesitation, the attorney pounced on my uncertainty. If I elaborated on an answer, he invariably found a way to make it seem as if I had contradicted myself. I left his office that day deeply shaken.

In the months leading up to the trial, I found myself waking in the night replaying the events that led to the lawsuit. What if we had done things differently? Should we have waited longer? Could we have taken another course and avoided this lawsuit altogether? And what if we lost the case? What then?

The insurance company was supposed to be our safety net. What if that net suddenly disappeared? For the first time in my life, I understood the plight of those people who find themselves entangled in the legal system. This was no longer a hypothetical drama played out on some TV show; this was happening to *me*.

After four and a half years of legal maneuvering, the case finally came to trial on the seventeenth floor of the Daley Center in downtown Chicago. For three days I sat for hours listening to testimony against me and the other defendants. The opposing attorneys used terms like *vigilante justice* and *witch-hunt* to make us look like criminals. As the days rolled on, it occurred to me how difficult it was to present things like church discipline in a purely secular setting. Issues that seem clear inside the church look different in a court of law.

A Shield Around Me

Finally, on the third day I took the stand. I remember feeling an enormous sense of foreboding as I walked to the witness chair. Then something quite amazing happened. I felt an invisible shield come down around me. In some way that I cannot fully explain, it felt as though an impenetrable shield had been lowered down from heaven. In that moment I felt invincible and untouchable. For the next twenty minutes as I answered each question, a sense of peace filled my soul. Then as I stood up to go back to my seat, I felt the shield lift from around me.

What had happened? I can't prove it, but I believe that the Lord sent His holy angels to be my protection at that critical moment. They were the "shield around me" that David mentions in Psalm 3:3.

When the plaintiffs finished presenting their case the next morning, our lawyer moved for a directed verdict, which means that he asked the judge to dismiss us from the case because no credible evidence had been presented against us. Naturally, the opposing lawyers vigorously argued against that motion. After thirty minutes of argument in the judge's chambers, our attorney came out and said he didn't know what was going to happen. When I asked him how often he had won a case on a directed verdict, he said it had happened three times in twenty years.

Absolutely, Positively Not Guilty

A directed verdict basically means this: When the plaintiff's case is considered in the most favorable light, and without any presentation at all by the defense, the plaintiff has so utterly failed to prove his case that no one can ever conclude that the defendants were guilty of the charges against them. When a judge grants a directed verdict, he is saying that this case should never have come to trial in the first place. It requires the highest standard of evidence in the American judicial system.

After deliberating for less than an hour, the judge granted the motion for a directed verdict, thus dismissing me and my staff member from the case. It was a complete vindication in the eyes of the law.

At some point I remember asking our lawyer how much this case had cost on both sides over the four and a half years since it had been filed. About $80,000, he estimated.

In an interesting twist, when we were dismissed from the case, the man who had filed the lawsuit against us actually came over and apologized and said that he knew we hadn't done anything wrong and that he was sorry for everything that had happened. Amazingly, we parted as friends, not enemies.

ADVERSITY IS ESSENTIAL

Looking back, I am still at a loss to explain why things happened the way they did. Yet I am sure that the many months of anxiety caused me to grow in my walk with the Lord. It certainly gave me compassion for those who feel trapped in the justice system. And I have a much deeper confidence in God's protection for His children—especially in moments of crisis. It certainly taught me that my security rests in God, and God alone.

That, I suppose, is the final reason God makes it hard when it ought to be easy. *He is developing character in us, and to do that, adversity is essential.* That is why life isn't easy, why nothing works the way it's supposed to, why we struggle so hard to get ahead. God's agenda and timetable are often quite different from ours.

In all of this we have the example of Jesus Christ, who "learned obedience from what he suffered" (Hebrews 5:8). If He had to learn obedience, how much more do we? If adversity was essential for the Son of God, how much more for us? So do not despair, my friend. The road is hard and the journey long because God made it that way. But there's a crown and throne at the end for those who persevere.

7

THE FEAR FACTOR

A few weeks ago my Promise Keepers group discussed a problem men rarely talk about. As is our custom, each man gave a report on how things were going in his life. We all laughed in sympathy as one man talked about the age-old problem called "What does my wife really want?" He said that his wife will sometimes say, "Why can't you be more like Gene?" referring to one of his good friends. When he repeated that comment to Gene, Gene replied that his wife sometimes says, "Why can't you be more like Phil?"

Then one man brought up the problem of anger. He told us how he had struggled with this issue over the years, even though most people have never seen him get angry. Heads nodded in agreement as he recounted how he sometimes takes frustration from his job home with him in the evening and takes it out on his family, which makes him feel worse, not better. Most men, we concluded, struggle with anger whether they admit it or not.

But what makes us angry? One answer kept surfacing. *Fear makes us angry.* That thought may sound strange when you first hear it. What does fear have to do with anger? Actually they are quite closely connected in that we often get angry because we fear the loss of control, or because we fear what others will think of us, or because we fear that our most cherished dreams won't come true.

What do you do when you have prayed and prayed and God still hasn't come through for you? If you are like most people, you begin to lose hope. And you wonder why you bothered to pray in the first place. Deep in the soil of your heart, little seeds of doubt take root, growing up into a harvest of frustration and anger.

It happens to most of us eventually. Even some of the best men and women of the Bible struggled with their inner doubts when their dreams didn't come true.

WAITING FOR A BABY

Abraham (Abram, Genesis 11:26–17:5) is a case in point. In order to understand his story, we have to go back forty centuries, back to a time long ago and far away, back to a place called Ur of the Chaldees, which was a large city on the banks of the Euphrates River. That river still exists. It flows through Iraq and empties into the Persian Gulf not far from Kuwait.

Historians tell us that Ur was one of the most important cities of the ancient world. In Abraham's day perhaps 250,000 people lived there. There was an ancient university in Ur and a large library. Ur was known as a center for mathematics, astronomy, and international commerce. It was like Chicago or New York or London or Singapore.

What else do we know about Abraham (Abram) as the story begins? He's about seventy-five years old when we meet him, which in those days would be considered middle-aged. He's a prosperous businessman who is no doubt well-known to many people. He is married to his wife Sarai (later called Sarah), and they have no children.

It is against that backdrop that God speaks to Abram for the first time in Genesis 12:1–3:

> The Lord had said to Abram, "Leave your country, your people and your father's household and go to the land I will show

you. I will make you into a great nation and I will bless you; I will make your name great and you will be a blessing. I will bless those who bless you, and whoever curses you I will curse; and all peoples on earth will be blessed through you."

Later God promised to give him descendants "like the dust of the earth" (Genesis 13:16). Ten years quickly pass without any sign of children. Abram is almost eighty-five and not getting any younger. His wife Sarai is far past child-bearing age. Even though he has just won a great victory (see Genesis 14), nothing can satisfy his deep desire for a son.

Only those who have gone through this experience can fully empathize with Abram and Sarai. There is no sadness like the sadness of wanting children of your own but being unable to have them. Even in this day of modern medicine and advanced technology, many couples wait for years and some couples wait forever. A few months ago I prayed with a wife who along with her husband has begged God for years for a child. By her own testimony she has tried every drug on the market and followed her doctor's advice meticulously. For some reason God has not yet answered her prayer. When I see her on Sunday, I see in her eyes the unspoken fear that perhaps He never will.

HAS GOD FORGOTTEN HIS PROMISE?

I think Abram's greatest fear stemmed from the fact that God did not seem in a hurry to give them a child. How much longer would He wait? Why had He delayed? Had God changed His mind and not told Abram? Was there some problem he didn't know about? Had they sinned? Were they doing something displeasing to God? Why was Sarai's womb still closed? If God had promised, why was it taking so long to be fulfilled? Should they go to Plan B?

All those questions were running through Abram's mind. God knew exactly what His servant was thinking. He saw the doubt. He understood the fear. Now He moves to reassure Abram that all will be well. The time has not yet come for the child to be born, but it isn't far off either.

"I AM YOUR SHIELD"

"After this, the word of the Lord came to Abram in a vision: 'Do not be afraid, Abram, I am your shield, your very great reward'" (Genesis 15:1).

There are at least four reasons Abram could have doubted God's promise of a son:

1. He was too old.
2. Too many years had passed since the promise had been given.
3. Nothing like this had ever happened before.
4. Sarah also doubted God's promise.

When you think about it, there was no reason to believe—no reason except that God had promised to do it. The question now is simple: Will God's promise be enough for Abraham?

In answer to that question, God declares, "I am your shield." We should not think of a small shield that covers only the chest area, but rather of a shield that stretches from head to toe and completely protects every part of the soldier's body. Such a shield offers complete protection from every attack of the enemy.

To call God our shield means two specific things:

1. He protects us in times of doubt.
2. He rescues us in times of danger.

A SHIELD AFTER MIDNIGHT

A few days ago I took a walk late in the afternoon. For

some reason I altered my normal route and headed east on Randolph, then north to the Dominick's store, walking along the alley, then back to South Street, crossing East Boulevard, until I came to Wesley Avenue. I turned left and began walking the two blocks back to my house at the corner of Wesley and Randolph. As I got within a half-block of my home I looked to my right and saw a tree with a large section of bark torn off near the bottom of the trunk. Someone had painted over the gash with a black substance. Then to my left I saw a green chain link fence slightly bent out of position. In a flash it all came back to me.

Late one night last summer my son and his friends had been driving our van when it jumped the curb, nearly hit a house, sideswiped the fence, jumped another curb, and hit the tree going fifty-five miles per hour. The van was totaled, all four people wound up in the hospital, and I was told later that it was a miracle that anyone walked away from the accident.

I cannot fully explain what happened that night or why my son and his friends were spared from sudden death. But I accept the words of my friend Howard Harvey, who said, "An angel took the hit."

As I walked past the spot for the first time since the accident, I felt like erecting a sign, "The Lord God is a shield around His people. He protects even in the darkness."

A CHRISTIAN IS IMMORTAL

I ran across the following quote one day: "A Christian is immortal 'till his work on earth is done." That statement means that *nothing can harm you without God's permission*. Not cancer, not AIDS, not bankruptcy, not theft, not physical disability, not the loss of your job, not a terrible accident, not the death of a child, not any of a thousand other sorrows that afflict the children of God. Christians aren't immune to sadness. What happens to others also happens to us. The difference is this: We know that God protects us from harm so that nothing can touch us that doesn't first pass through His hands of love.

That knowledge doesn't meant that we don't weep or we don't suffer. Far from it. But it is the basis for the statement that "we sorrow but not as those who have no hope" (see 1 Thessalonians 4:13). Our sorrow is different precisely because we hope in God.

"Nothing Except That Which My God Permits"

During a recent trip overseas I met a missionary who told me how she had nearly been put in jail. It turned out that about ten years ago a hostile lawyer began harassing her and the local Christian hospital. He objected to the fact that the hospital openly did evangelism along with its compassionate medical care.

Seeking a pretext for legal action, the lawyer accused the hospital of illegally selling intravenous fluid to its patients. It wasn't true, but that didn't matter. For nearly ten years the case bumped up and down the court system of that country. At one point several years ago it appeared likely that the missionary might either be thrown in jail or forced to leave the country. "I'm going to shut down this hospital," the lawyer chortled, "And you're going to jail or I'll have you deported."

To which the missionary replied, "You can do nothing to me except what my God permits you to do."

That's a perfectly biblical answer. Our God is a shield around His people. Nothing can touch us except that which God permits.

Why God Delays His Answers

That brings us back to the central issue of this chapter. Why did God wait so long to give Abraham a son? Abraham was seventy-five when God first spoke to him and one hundred when Isaac was finally born. He was almost eighty-five when God came to him and said, "Fear not." After all these years God still wasn't ready to answer Abraham's prayers. Abraham was old, but he would be older yet before Isaac was finally born.

Of all the questions that plague the people of God, none is so vexing as the question of unanswered prayer. We know God loves us and has a good plan for our lives. *Why then does God take so long to answer our deepest, most heartfelt prayers?* From Abraham's experience we may suggest three answers:

1. To develop in us the quality of perseverance.

To put it very simply, it would be too easy if God answered all our prayers the first time we prayed them. Not only would we take God for granted, we would also develop a shallow faith.

I have a good friend who is stuck in a difficult job situation. She works with a colleague who has a reputation for being an easygoing nice guy. "But he's not like that behind the scenes," she says. Every time she has a good idea, he either steals it or complains to the boss. And since his job is more important than hers, he always wins. He also uses threats and intimidation to get his way. He thinks only of himself and how he can get ahead, and he doesn't mind being ruthless if that's what it takes to get what he wants.

Sound familiar? Every office probably has a person who answers to that description. When I asked my friend if she was planning on leaving her job, she gave a very wise answer: "I know that God put me here and gave me the talent to do my job. If He wants to move me, that's fine, but I'm not going to try to do it myself. I'm sure God can use me in this position and I want to learn everything He is trying to teach me."

Here is a woman whose faith is growing stronger through a difficult situation. Every day she is being given new opportunities to trust God and to respond graciously to an unkind coworker. Meanwhile, she prays for God to work in her and through her and, if necessary, to change her situation.

My own feeling is that God will eventually answer her prayers by either moving her on to a new job or by removing the other person. But that may not happen for months or years, and until then, my friend is developing many godly qualities as she patiently waits on the Lord.

2. So that when the answer comes no one but God can get the glory.

When Paul wrote about Abraham's story, he mentioned this point prominently. Romans 4:19–21 says,

> Without weakening in his faith, he faced the fact that his body was as good as dead—since he was about a hundred years old—and that Sarah's womb was also dead. Yet he did not waver through unbelief regarding the promise of God, but was strengthened in his faith and *gave glory to God*, being fully persuaded that God had power to do what he had promised (italics added).

Not only did Abraham have to wait twenty-five years for an answer to his prayers, he also had to suffer the humiliation of his own failed schemes. Immediately after God spoke to him in Genesis 15, he agreed with Sarah to sleep with their maidservant Hagar in hope of conceiving a child through her. It worked, and Ishmael was born. But this shortsighted attempt to "help God out" backfired and brought sadness and heartache to everyone involved.

God often delays His answers so that we will have plenty of opportunity to fail using our own resources. Only then does God act, but when He does, it demonstrates that He alone is responsible for answering our prayers and that He alone must get the glory.

3. **To give hope to everyone who has prayed and prayed for years without receiving an answer.**

I think that's why Hebrews 11 gives more space to Abraham's story than to any other Old Testament hero. He is the preeminent man of faith in the Bible. When we read his story and see how long he waited (twenty-five years), we gain a new perspective on our own situation.

If Abraham had to wait, it should not surprise us that we will often have to wait a long time for the fulfillment of our dreams and the answers to our prayers. And as with Abraham, waiting is not bad if it causes us to deepen our trust in God and to learn more about His character.

THE ANSWER IS A PERSON

God's answer to fear is not an argument or a formula. It's a Person. That's why He said to Abraham, "Fear not. I am your shield." God Himself is the final answer to every fear of the human heart.

Have you ever wondered why God called Himself by the name "I AM" in the Old Testament? Certainly it has to do with His eternal existence, but there is also a word of personal encouragement in that name.

Think of it this way. Who is God to you? According to His name, He is the essence of whatever you need at the moment.

> I am your strength.
> I am your courage.
> I am your health.
> I am your hope.
> I am your supply.
> I am your defender.
> I am your deliverer.
> I am your forgiveness.
> I am your joy.
> I am your future.

In short, God is saying to you and me, *"I am whatever you need whenever you need it."* He is the all-sufficient God for every crisis.

MOVING FROM FEAR TO FAITH

Let's wrap up this chapter by looking at four principles that will move us from fear to faith.

1. Fear focuses on the past; faith focuses on the future.

A woman struggling with personal issues of fear and doubt told me that she had changed her phone number and left it unlisted. In some ways you might say she is gripped with fear as she thinks about certain people and what they might do to her. As we talked together, I finally looked her in the eye and said, "It's time to move from fear to faith. Are you ready to move with me?" She smiled hesitantly and then said yes. We prayed, claiming God's promises of protection. When I saw her the next day she said that she had slept much better that night because she wasn't focusing on her fears.

Think of Abraham. The past argued against his ever having a child. So did the present. His only hope lay in the promises of God for the future. As long as he looked back, he would never have faith to believe God. His only hope was to step out into the future, trusting that somehow, someway God would keep His promises.

2. Faith means trusting in God's timing—not your own.

So many of our struggles with fear start right here. Deep down, we fear that God has somehow made a mistake in His dealings with us. Like Abraham, we have waited and waited—sometimes for years on end. Even though we may have seen many remarkable answers to prayer, the one thing that means the most to us has not been granted.

As I write these words I am thinking of certain people I know who pray faithfully week after week for their loved ones to be saved. Some of them write notes each week asking prayer for an unsaved husband or wife. Week in and week out the requests come in and the staff prays for them faithfully. One husband has been praying for his wife for seven years with no real change in sight. Another wife faithfully requests prayer for her husband. Sometimes he seems interested in spiritual things, then his interest suddenly seems to disappear.

I know a man whose wife converted to Christ from Judaism over twenty years ago. For reasons that aren't entirely clear, she recently gave up her Christian faith and returned to a local synagogue. Is she just confused? Is she searching for her own identity? When will she come back to Jesus? Her husband doesn't have a clue and doesn't know where to begin looking for answers. But he prays earnestly for his wife day and night.

Where is God? Why doesn't He answer the fervent, heartfelt prayers of His people?

Of the many answers that might be given to that question, one answer must be that *God's timing and ours are often quite different.* Sometimes we are living in eastern daylight saving time and God seems to be working in Pacific daylight saving time.

3. Faith grows by believing God in spite of your circumstances.

Sometimes our circumstances make it easy to believe in God; other times we have to struggle. As I write these words my dear friend Stan Utigard battles with cancer. He is one of the finest men I know; a man whose gentle spirit endears him to others. I got to know him on a golf retreat when we shared a round and a few jokes. That weekend he pulled out his harmonica and played hymns and a few western songs. He and his wife Marge celebrated their fiftieth wedding anniversary several years ago. But the news from the doctors is not good. The cancer is not operable, nor is it curable.

No one knows how much time he has left, but that doesn't seem to matter to him. When I talked with him a few weeks ago, he spoke about the goodness of God. He added that he and Marge had had a long and happy life together and they knew that God would take care of them. Not long after that he and Marge wrote a note that appeared in our church newsletter thanking everyone for their prayers. It ended with this sentence: "No matter what happens we are trusting in the Lord." That's biblical faith rising above its circumstances to lay hold of the eternal promises of God.

4. Faith is obeying God one step at a time and leaving the future in His hands.

This principle is often overlooked by those seeking to do God's will. God promised a child and Abraham desperately wanted to see the fulfillment of that promise. So what does God tell him to do? Round up the animals for a sacrifice (see Genesis 15:9–11). How do you get from there to the nursery? Abraham doesn't have a clue and God doesn't tell him a thing. But Abraham now has a choice. He can choose to obey God, round up the animals, and get ready for a sacrifice, even though it doesn't seem to connect with the son of his dreams. Or he can argue with God or decide to take matters in his own hands.

How often we stumble over this. We slight the near in favor of the far, shirking the duties of today because we are dreaming about some distant tomorrow. But until we have done what God has called us to do today, we will never be prepared for what He wants us to do tomorrow.

In the end 99 percent of life turns out to be humdrum, ordinary routine. It's the same old thing day after day. *Yet out of the humdrum God is weaving an unseen pattern that will one day lead us in a new direction.* Faith means taking the next step—whatever it is—and walking with God wherever He leads us. Sometimes it will make sense, other times it won't. But we still have to take that step if we are going to do God's will.

CAN YOU TRUST GOD?

Everything I've been trying to say in this chapter comes down to one simple question: *Can God be trusted to do what is right?* More and more I am convinced that this is the fundamental question of life. If the answer is yes, then we can face the worst that life has to offer. If the answer is no, then we're no better off than the people who have no faith at all. In fact, if the answer is no or if we're not sure, then we really don't have any faith anyway.

Not long ago while doing a radio interview, I was asked how I could be so positive and confident when I spoke about God's will. The man asking the question seemed burdened with many cares and difficulties. My answer went this way:

> Twenty-three years ago when my father died, I came face to face with the ultimate unanswerable question of life. I didn't know then why such a good man would have to die at the young age of fifty-six or why he would leave my mother and her four sons without a husband and a father. I had no clue about what God was doing. In the years since then I have learned many things about life, but I confess that I still don't understand why my father died. It doesn't make any more sense to me now than it did then. I am older and wiser, but in the one question that really matters I have no answers. But I have learned since then that faith is a choice you make. *Sometimes you choose to believe because of what you see; often you believe in spite of what you can see.*
>
> As I look to the world around me, many things remain mysterious and unanswerable. But if there is no God, and if He is not good, then nothing at all makes sense. *I have chosen*

to believe because I must believe. I truly have no other choice. If I sound confident, it is only because I have learned through my tears that my only confidence is in God and God alone.

My older brother Andy is a urologist who recently lost a twenty-year-old patient to a rare form of kidney cancer. When he asked me in all seriousness, "Why did he die?" I had no answer. But I felt no shame in saying that. I have decided to believe that God is good and can be trusted no matter what happens. If I didn't believe that, I wouldn't have the strength to get out of bed every day.

"BUT I CAN TRUST"

Pioneer missionary J. Hudson Taylor founded the China Inland Mission one hundred years ago. During the terrible days of the Boxer Rebellion, when missionaries were being captured and killed, he went through such agony of soul that he could not pray. Writing in his journal, he summarized his spiritual condition this way: "I can't read. I can't think. I can't pray. But I can trust."

There will be times when we can't read the Bible. Sometimes we won't be able to focus our thoughts on God at all. Often we will not even be able to pray. But in those moments when we can't do anything else, we can still trust in the loving purposes of our heavenly Father.

Fear not, child of God. No one knows what a day may bring. Who knows if we will all make it through this week? But our God is faithful to keep every one of His promises. Nothing can happen to us except it first passes through the hands of God. If your way is dark, keep on believing. His eye is on the sparrow, and I know He cares for you.

8

QUESTIONS
AND ANSWERS

Whenever we go through hard times we have many questions about God, about good and evil, and about how we can respond to the trials of life. In this chapter we will address some of the common questions asked by those who want to keep on believing in spite of hard times.

Question: Why is there so much suffering and evil in the world?

Answer: This question is both difficult and simple. Or it is easy and impossible. Suffering and evil come as a by-product of sin in the universe. Romans 5:12 tells us that death came into the world as a result of sin. Romans 8:20–22 speaks of all creation being in bondage to decay. In a world without sin, there would be no death, no pain, no suffering, no loss, no senility, no sickness, and no suffering.

Even as I write those words, I hardly believe them because I simply cannot imagine a world without pain and death. But God did not create the world with a bent toward its own destruction. Man added that particular feature all by himself.

Once Adam ate the forbidden fruit, sin entered the human bloodstream and has remained there until this very day. From that one act of disobedience has come a river of evil, pain, and death. That river still flows throughout the world, touching everyone born on the planet.

The impossible part of the question deals with the ultimate "Why?" behind sin. Why did God create a universe where Adam's sin could take place? How could God allow such suffering in the world He created? The greatest minds have probed these questions over the centuries. The Christian answer includes these elements: First, although God permitted sin, He Himself is not morally guilty of sin. Second, God will ultimately be glorified through every decision He has made, including the decision to permit sin in the first place. Third, God has offered the ultimate solution to the "sin problem" by offering His own Son as the ultimate sacrifice for sin. Fourth, giving man free will also meant giving him the freedom to do wrong.

Question: Do you believe in miraculous healing through prayer?

Answer: I believe that God can and sometimes does heal through means that seem to be miraculous. Certainly the Lord Jesus often worked miracles of healing through His Word and through His touch. No one who reads the Gospels can doubt the mighty power of the Lord. Furthermore, I am not able to find any clear statement in Scripture that indicates that God cannot or will not work in miracles today when it is according to His will. He *can* work miracles and He *does* when it is according to His divine plan.

Yet not everyone we pray for is healed. Some stay sick for months and others eventually die. And even those who are healed die sooner or later. This is one of those hard facts that we must all face sooner or later. Every Christian funeral testifies to the fact that the "last enemy" that will be destroyed is death (see 1 Corinthians 15:26). Like all pastors, I have performed my share of heartbreaking funeral services for believers who died in spite of the fervent prayers of many people.

So whatever else we may say about miraculous healing, it doesn't happen all the time, and it doesn't happen as often as we wish it would.

But it does happen, or at least as a pastor, I have seen some cases of dramatic recovery that seemed to be beyond normal medical explanation. During my days as a younger pastor, I was approached by a woman who asked if I would anoint her with oil and pray for her healing. The thought was entirely new to me since the church I grew up in did not do such things, nor had I received any training for this in seminary. But the woman's request was biblical, being based on James 5:14–15:

> Is any one of you sick? He should call the elders of the church to pray over him and anoint him with oil in the name of the Lord. And the prayer offered in faith will make the sick person well; the Lord will raise him up. If he has sinned, he will be forgiven.

There are several points worth noting. First, the call comes from the sick person who feels the need for prayer. Second, the elders are to gather at the sick person's bedside and literally pray "over" him. Third, anointing with oil has no curative power in itself but must be done "in the name of the Lord." Fourth, God must Himself grant the faith to believe that the healing will take place. Both the faith and the healing come from the Lord. Fifth, the prayer is offered in view of healing without regard to the means of healing. This means that the prayer should not be offered as a substitute for medical care but in conjunction with the best medical advice available at the time. Sixth, since sickness can sometimes be the result of sin, healing will not come until those sins are honestly confessed and forsaken.

I can truthfully say that I had not thought through all this when the woman came asking for prayer. Years earlier she had undergone one of the first heart bypass operations. Now her arteries had become like chalk and she had a severe blockage in her lower abdomen. Because of her frail condition the doctors were reluctant to operate. Would we pray for a reversal of the blockage?

I will never forget meeting with this dear woman in my office after a Sunday morning service. Several of my elders listened with me as she told her story. Not knowing what else to do, I read James 5:14–15, asked her if she had any sins to confess, then I dipped my finger in olive oil and dabbed a bit on her forehead. One by one the elders and I prayed for God to heal her. As we did so we were all aware of a powerful sense of God's presence that filled the room.

Two days later she called me with wonderful news. Upon returning to her doctor, she was told that her blockage had entirely disappeared and that surgery would not be necessary. We all rejoiced upon hearing the good report. We knew that God had answered our prayers.

That was my first experience in praying for the sick according to James 5:14–15. In the years since then I have repeated that simple procedure many different times with many different people suffering from many different ailments. I wish I could tell you that each time I have prayed the person has been healed, but that would not be true. Often I have experienced that same sense of God's presence and often individuals have reported improvement in their conditions. But those reports have generally come when prayer has been combined with compassionate medical treatment.

And sometimes I have prayed for dear friends to be healed from cancer and other diseases only to discover that I would later officiate at their funerals. I suppose every pastor could say the same thing.

One other note. I hadn't heard a thing about the woman we prayed for until a few months ago when I heard that she had died of congestive heart failure. So even though I believe she was healed in answer to prayer, she eventually died because death is still "the last enemy" of the people of God.

Whenever anyone asks my theology of healing, I tell them very simply, "We do the praying and God does the healing—in His own time, in His own way, according to His own will."

Question: But why are some people healed in answer to prayer and others not healed?

Answer: Either I could write another book to answer that question or I could say very simply, I don't know. Sometimes we may be able to discern lessons God may be teaching through sickness, but other times we must simply stand silent before a mighty God whose ways are past finding out.

I suppose that some people would say that if healing does not take place it is because someone lacked faith. But whose faith are we talking about? The sick person's? The ones doing the praying? If you believe, as I do, that faith itself is a gift from God (Ephesians 2:8), then I believe that God will grant that kind of faith for those instances where He is pleased to also grant healing.

But someone may object that to say it that way simply rolls the problem back on God. True, but I would rather roll the problem on Him than attempt to place such a burden on mortal men and women. He can bear all our burdens, including the burden of all our unanswered questions.

Question: What happens when we die?

Answer: It depends on what happens before you die. Those who have trusted Jesus Christ as Savior go immediately into the presence of the Lord. They are "away from the body and at home with the Lord" (2 Corinthians 5:8). As the apostle Paul languished in a Roman jail, he expressed a desire to depart from his earthly body and to be with Christ in heaven. In his mind, dying would be gain because it would usher him into the personal presence of Jesus Christ (Philippians 1:21–23). Jesus made the same promise to the thief on the cross: "Today you will be with me in paradise" (Luke 23:43).

Meanwhile the body is buried awaiting the day of resurrection. First Thessalonians 4:13–18 tells us that when Jesus returns to the earth the "dead in Christ" will rise first. That means there will be literal resurrection of the bodies of believers who died "in Christ." That resurrection will be no less literal and no less physical than Jesus' own resurrection.

Often while conducting a graveside service I will remind those present of the words Moses said when he heard the voice coming from the burning bush: "Take off your sandals, for the place where you are standing is holy ground" (Exodus 3:5). Then I will say something like this: "This place of burial is holy ground. Look around you. Today all you see are signs of death. Gravestones, markers, flowers, monuments. Everything about this place is quiet, peaceful, serene. It is a good place to bury the dead. But it won't always be like this. When Jesus returns, this very spot will be a place of resurrection. Take off your shoes, you are standing on resurrection ground."

But what happens to those who die without Jesus Christ? They are sent immediately into a place of torment called hell. They will remain there until the Great White Throne judgment when they will be condemned for all eternity and cast into the lake of fire (Luke 16:19–31; Revelation 20:11–15).

If these things are true, then the most important decision you can ever make is the decision to trust Jesus Christ as Lord and Savior. And the most important thing you can ever do for your friends and loved ones is to share the good news that Jesus died and rose again and wants to be their Savior.

Question: Will we know one another in heaven?

Answer: The answer from Scripture seems to be yes, but not in the same sense we know each other on earth. When Jesus was transfigured on the mountain, the Bible says that Moses and Elijah appeared with Him and actually engaged Him in a conversation (Luke 9:30). At this moment in history, Moses had already been dead for some 1,400 years and Elijah had been taken up into heaven 850 years earlier (Deuteronomy 34:5–6; 2 Kings 2:11–12, 15–18). Yet they both retained conscious existence after death. And Peter, James, and John immediately recognized them.

It's also useful to recall that in the story Jesus told about the rich man and Lazarus, the rich man in hell recognized Lazarus, who was at Abraham's side in heaven (Luke 16:19–31). This seems to indicate that memory survives death intact. He also recognized Abraham, who had lived hundreds of years earlier.

Luke 20:27–40 sheds more light on this question. When the Sadducees came with a question about a woman with seven husbands, Jesus replied by noting that those who are raised from the dead "will neither marry nor be given in marriage" (v. 35). This means that many of the associations of this life will not continue in the same form throughout eternity.

But that's not all of Jesus' answer. He then referred to the words of God in Exodus 3:6 when He told Moses, "I am . . . the God of Abraham, the God of Isaac, and the God of Jacob." In Luke Jesus was arguing from the standpoint of the tense of a verb. God didn't say, "I *was* the God of Abraham," but "I *am* the God of Abraham," meaning that as far as Jesus was concerned, Abraham, Isaac, and Jacob were still alive in God's presence. "He is not the God of the dead, but of the living, for to him all are alive" (Luke 20:38).

So will we know one another in heaven? The answer would seem to be yes, but it won't be like the knowing on earth. Now we see through a glass darkly, but then we will see face to face. *Our knowing will be deeper, better, richer, more intimate, because we will know each other as God made us to know each other, without the stain of sin and the taint of a fallen nature.*

In that day we will know each other so well and our delight in each other will be so deep that the dearest friendships of this life will seem as if we never really knew each other at all. In heaven there will be no strangers.

Question: I've been going through many trials lately. How can I discover what God is saying to me through these hard times?

Answer: Often we won't be able to discern any particular message from a particular trial while we are going through it. Sometimes we won't see a purpose for our hardships until they are through and we can look back and see God's hand at work. And sometimes even then the things we have endured will make no sense.

In those cases we must go back to the words of Scripture. Job 23:10 tells us, "But he knows the way that I take; when he has tested me, I will come forth as gold." The first part of the verse is the key to the second part. God knows what you are going through right now. He sees it and knows, for before the beginning of time He ordained this trial for you. It has not happened to you by "chance" or "luck" or "fate" or "cruel misfortune." Do not fall into the trap of believing those worldly explanations. The old expression "Into each life some rain must fall" reveals an important truth. No one gets an easy road to heaven. Though the price of entry has been paid with the blood of Christ, the road we must travel on earth is filled with "many dangers, toils and snares."

Therefore, we must not be surprised when a multitude

of "fiery trials" come our way—sometimes one after another and sometimes two or three at the same time. God sends trials as part of His plan to bring us to maturity, to conform us to the image of Christ, and to cause us to "come forth as gold."

Many years ago I worked in a factory that produced soft-drink bottles. Once the molten glass was forced into the mold, a perfectly shaped bottle emerged and began traveling down the assembly line. It immediately went into an oven, which baked the bottle at an extremely high temperature for about ten minutes. One night I saw the foreman take a newly molded bottle from the assembly line before it had gone into the oven. When he poured water on it, the bottle shattered. He explained that unless the bottle had been "tempered" by the hot oven, it would shatter under the slightest pressure. But once tempered, it could withstand high-pressure bottling.

The same is true for you and me. The trials of life "temper" us and make us stronger. As painful as they are, those trials are actually gifts from God—even though we never think so when we are in middle of a hard time.

The truth is, you will often not know why God sends a particular trial at a particular time, but you can rest assured that God makes no mistakes and in the end will produce gold in your life.

Question: After twenty-five years of marriage, my husband left me for a younger woman. In the divorce papers he accused me of being an alcoholic and mentally unstable. I prayed and prayed for God to save my marriage, but now I am divorced. How can I get over my anger toward my ex-husband and toward God?

Answer: Your pain is very real and nothing I can say will reduce your suffering or the humiliation you have experienced at the hands of the one person you trusted more than anyone else in the whole world. Your husband not only broke his vows, he also broke your heart and destroyed your reputation. Now you have the burden of facing life alone knowing that he is living with the other woman.

But your greater problem comes from the silence of God. Where was He when your husband walked out? Why didn't He intervene to stop the lies? Even though you asked Him to change your husband's heart, He didn't do it. Even worse, it almost seems as if your husband has gotten away with adultery and smeared your name in the process. How could God allow such a thing?

In the first place, it's important to remember that God is with you right now. He never left you during all your suffering, and He is with you in this moment even though you feel entirely alone. He said, "I will never leave you," and He won't. Second, remember that God gave your husband free will, and he willfully chose to do wrong. Third, you now face an all-important choice. No one in life can stay in one place forever. Either you decide to go back and live in the past, dwelling on the hurts of yesterday and building up walls of anger and resentment, or you choose by faith to let them go.

Not long ago I attended a banquet and sat next to a woman who reported with some excitement that she had just heard a wonderful lecture on the subject of mental toughness. The thought intrigued me, so I asked her to share the speaker's key idea. The speaker had indicated that the key to mental toughness is focusing on the present. The people who survive great problems in life are the ones who focus narrowly on the task at hand. They don't dwell in the past or worry about the future. They simply do whatever has to be done at any given moment.

This is excellent advice for anyone who has been deeply hurt. Each and every day you must begin by saying, "Lord, it's You and me today, and even if no one else comes along to help out, I'm trusting You completely. Help me to do Your will without living in the past or dreaming about the future."

Question: That sounds good, but how do I get over my anger toward my ex-husband?

Answer: You need to know that anger is not always sinful. Ephesians 4:26 says, "In your anger do not sin." In your case, you have every right to be angry about the way your ex-husband treated you. It's not surprising that you will sometimes find yourself consumed with angry thoughts toward him. But again, the question is whether or not you will choose to continue living that way.

God has a one-word answer for the problem of deep-seated anger and bitterness. It's called forgiveness. I can almost hear you objecting as I write these words, "But how can I forgive him after what he did to me?" That's a good question but it's not the right question. Since God Himself commands you to practice forgiveness and since the Lord's Prayer even says, "Forgive us our debts, as we also have forgiven our debtors" (Matthew 6:12), the real question is, "How can I do what God asks me to do?"

The most important truth to know is that forgiveness is an act of the heart. You forgive by a conscious choice of your will. You must choose to forgive your husband in spite of what he did to you. In this case, forgiveness means consciously choosing not to dwell in the past, not to constantly repeat the sordid story of what he did, and actively deciding you will move forward by faith, letting go of the bitter feelings one by one.

This isn't easy, and it won't happen overnight, and you will probably need the help of some good friends who can help you talk through your feelings and hold you accountable to move forward and not backward. But it can be done.

In one of her books Corrie ten Boom tells of some Christian friends who wronged her in a public and malicious way. For many days, she was bitter and angry until she forgave them. But in the night she would wake up thinking about what they had done and she would get angry all over again. It seemed the memory would not go away.

Help came from her Lutheran pastor to whom she confessed her frustration after two sleepless weeks. He told her, "Corrie, up in the church tower is a bell which is rung by pulling on a rope. When the sexton pulls the rope, the bells peal out ding-dong, ding-dong, ding-dong. But if he doesn't keep pulling on the rope, the sound slowly fades away. *Forgiveness is like that. When we forgive someone, we take our hand off the rope.* But if we've been tugging at our grievances for a long time, we mustn't be surprised if the old angry thoughts keep coming for a while. They are just the ding-dongs of the old bell slowing down."

So it's not surprising if after forgiveness, the memories keep coming back for a while. If you refuse to dwell on them, slowly they will fade away. Why? *When you forgive, you let go of the rope and the force is gone out of your anger.*

Question: The son of my best friend recently died in an automobile accident. Now she blames herself for his death even though she had nothing to do with the accident. How can I help my friend through this crisis?

Answer: The very best thing you can do is simply to be there for her. Proverbs 17:17 says, "A friend loves at all times, and a brother is born for adversity." Your friend will never forget that you cared enough to spend time with her during her darkest days. Remember, too, that Job's friends helped him more during the seven days they were silent than when they finally started talking. It's OK not to have all the answers. Assure your friend that you love her and that God loves her. As you have the opportunity, gently remind her that God will not hold her responsible for her son's death. Point her toward the cross, where God's own Son died for the sins of the world. She needs to know that God knows what she is going through. He's been there because He watched

His Son die on a bloody Roman cross—and that was no accident, but the treacherous act of sinful men.

Finally, give your friend the time and space she needs to go through the grieving process. Her life will never be the same, and she will need your friendship more now than ever before.

Question: I'm afraid of dying. How can I overcome my fear of death?

Answer: First of all, you have nothing to be ashamed of. Millions of people share your fear of death and dying. Sometimes the fear of dying has more to do with the possible pain and suffering associated with death. And it is certainly true you may die in a way that is unpleasant or even painful. Most of us won't be able to orchestrate the time and place of our own deaths, and we normally won't be able to completely control the circumstances.

At that point we are faced once again with the central question of this book: Do we believe that God is in control and that He is good and has our best interests at heart? If God is in control, then we may rest assured that He has numbered our days from the beginning to the end and that our life rests safely in His hands. That doesn't mean that we are immune to sudden death, cancer, or a lingering, painful death. But it does mean that we don't have to live in abject fear of those things. Hebrews 2:15 tells us that Jesus came to "free those who all their lives were held in slavery by their fear of death." Because He died and rose from the dead, He can set us free from overwhelming fear.

One of my college professors mentioned in class that her aunt was at the point of death and was struggling with her feelings of fear and personal failure. I remember that the professor said she was praying that God would give her aunt "dying grace." The term is a bit old-fashioned today, but it perfectly describes one special ministry of the Holy Spirit. I believe He is able to give the children of God special comfort and a sense of abiding peace in the last hours of life on earth.

Someone once asked John Wesley what made his followers so different from others. "Our people die well," he replied. Indeed, Christians of all people ought to "die well," for we have the assurance of eternal life through Jesus Christ. And that thought brings us full circle back to your question. Do you know Jesus Christ as Lord and Savior? Have you ever committed yourself to Him completely and without reservation? If the answer is no or if you are not sure, I urge you to place your trust in Him without delay. God's answer to your fear of death is His Son who conquered death on your behalf.

Question: Although I was raised in the church as a child, somewhere along the way I lost my faith. Now that I am older I am trying to find something to believe in but don't know where to begin. Can you help me?

Answer: I am happy to tell you that you are in excellent shape for a new beginning. The first step in changing your life is always to admit that things really do need to change. Your story reminds me of so many people who were raised in Christian homes, but somewhere along the way they drifted away from the Lord and from the church.

Sometimes we make our quest for faith too difficult. Jesus instructed us to have the faith of a child if we truly want to know God. "I tell you the truth, unless you change and become like little children, you will never enter the kingdom of heaven" (Matthew 18:3). Think of the faith of a child. What words come to mind? Innocence, simplicity, humility, honesty. Above all else, a little child has a trusting heart. He believes because no one has ever given him a reason not to believe.

You once had that kind of faith but now it has disappeared. May I recommend three simple steps? First, go back to the Bible and begin reading it again. It doesn't really matter where you begin, but each day set aside a few minutes to let God speak to you personally through His Word. Second, begin each day with this prayer: "Lord Jesus, I come to you as a little child. Help me to grow in my faith as I walk with You today. Amen." Third, tell at least three people this week that you are on a journey to rediscover your faith in God. Sharing that fact will strengthen your resolve and it may also challenge them to do the same.

Finally, don't feel like you have to have all your questions answered. Come to Christ with childlike confidence and He will give you the faith to believe again.

Question: I feel like a failure. Recently I lost my job when the company decided that they no longer needed my services. They said it was nothing personal, but I feel like a loser anyway. What do I do now?

Answer: Don't give up. You're not the first person ever to lose his job. And you're not the first person ever to feel like a failure. If we're honest, all of us have experienced some kind of failure. We've all been rejected, passed over, flunked out, cut from the team, or otherwise made to feel that we somehow aren't needed or wanted. Failure is simply a part of life, and the longer we live, the more opportunity we have to fail.

Failure is the most democratic of all clubs, admitting old and young, rich and poor, men and women. About the only thing its members have in common is their secrecy about belonging. Think what a national convention of all eligible members of the Failure Club would look like—millions of people crowded tightly together in thousands of rooms across America—all looking down at their feet.

I have three pieces of good news for you. First, the Bible records the stories of many abysmal failures. Abraham lied about his wife, Moses killed a man, David committed adultery, and Peter denied Christ. These were some of the greatest men in the Bible, yet their failures are recorded for all the world to see.

Second, God specializes in helping failures find a new start in life. After all, that's what salvation is all about. Until you admit that you are a failure, you can never be saved. In that sense we're all failures because all of us have sinned against a holy God. Since only sinners can be saved, the only people in heaven will be those with the courage to admit they failed while on the earth.

Third, failure doesn't have to be final. Did you know that Abraham Lincoln struck out eleven times before he was elected President?

> He failed in business in 1831.
>
> He was defeated for the legislature in 1832.
>
> He had his second business failure in 1833.
>
> He suffered a nervous breakdown in 1836.
>
> He was defeated for Speaker in 1838.
>
> Defeated for Elector in 1840.
>
> Defeated for Congress in 1843.
>
> Defeated for Congress in 1848.
>
> Defeated for the Senate in 1855.
>
> Defeated for vice president in 1856.
>
> Defeated for the Senate in 1858.
>
> Elected president in 1860.

Yet no one thinks of Lincoln as a failure. Failure doesn't have to be final unless you decide to make it that way.

One final thought. God expects more failure from you than you expect from yourself.

God knows we're going to fail—and He is not surprised when we do. This is very freeing, for it means that He still loves us and cares for us. Our acceptance is not based upon our performance.

When Jesus told Peter, "Follow me!" (John 21:19), He was showing him the way back from failure and defeat. Remember, He knows you're going to fail. When it comes right down to it, the important thing is whether or not you are going to follow Him. Jesus can help restore your hope—He can give you the desire to get back up—if you will follow Him. Jesus never failed, but He loves failures like you and me.

9

WHAT MR. DUFLOTH WOULD LIKE TO KNOW

His name was Tom Dufloth. He was our next-door neighbor for nearly five years when we lived in California. We never knew him as well as we knew the rest of his family. Marlene knew his wife, and we all knew his three daughters. Tom was a salesman of some kind, and we would see him come buzzing up to his home in a little red sports car. His wife worked as a waitress in a local restaurant. The girls were about ten, eight, and six years old when we first met them.

Over the years we became casual friends. Never close friends, but the kind you would speak to when you happened to see them out in the yard. Once Marlene helped the girls bake a cake for their mom's birthday. It was that kind of friendship.

We never talked much about religion. Tom and his wife knew I was a pastor, and they were happy for the girls to come to church with us occasionally. As far as I know, they didn't have a church home.

What has happened to them in the intervening years? I

really have no idea. I'm not sure I would even recognize them if they walked through the door. They were neighbors, casual friends, decent people. The kind of family that probably lives next door to you.

You know their names, don't you? They're the Smiths or the Gravellis or the Gonzalezes or the Johnsons or the Pearsons or the Washingtons or the Hesters or the Bergmans or the Thorntons. Nice people. Friendly to you. You smile when you see them, and you say, "How's it going?" Occasionally you stop and chat for a while. You talk about the weather, your kids, your vacation plans, that sort of thing. Once in a great while you might go over to their home—but not very often. Sometimes you don't see them for several weeks, and then you might see them four days in a row.

Our country is full of Dufloths and Smiths and Andersons, and they all have problems of one kind or another. You don't have to be best friends to find that out. Next-door neighbors will do just fine.

Lately I've been thinking about the Dufloths. To me they represent all the next-door neighbors on every street in every town in America. They are good and decent people who don't go to church very often and who know almost nothing about Jesus Christ. I've been meditating on the question: What is it that Mr. Dufloth would like to know which, if he knew it, would make a difference in his life?

I think there are three things he would like to know about Jesus Christ. I stumbled across them as I was meditating on a verse of Scripture in the book of Revelation. The verse is Revelation 1:5. To a casual reader it would not appear to offer anything Mr. Dufloth would like to know. But I am persuaded otherwise.

Actually, this verse is part of the introduction to the book of Revelation. It is part of the greeting, where the apostle John introduces himself and wishes his readers grace and peace, and it is the apostle's description of Jesus Christ:

"Who is the faithful witness, the firstborn from the dead, and the ruler of the kings of the earth."

In this passage are three titles of Christ, each one touching something the men and women of this generation would like to know. If you will, each title answers a question Mr. Dufloth would like to ask about Jesus Christ.

CAN I TRUST HIM?

The first question is the most basic of all. The men and women of this generation have heard the name of Jesus many times. What they want to know is very simple: *Can I trust Him?* In a world of religious charlatans, this is where we must begin. The answer is found in John's first title. He calls Jesus "the faithful witness." A witness is one who tells what he has seen or heard. A faithful witness is one whose testimony is reliable every time.

John is saying that Jesus Christ can be relied upon to tell the truth. When He speaks, He speaks only the truth. This is one of the great themes John comes back to again and again: that Jesus Christ is a faithful witness whose word is absolutely true and authoritative. First Timothy 6:13 speaks of "Christ Jesus, who while testifying before Pontius Pilate made the good confession." And what did He say when he stood before Pilate? "I came into the world to testify to the truth. Everyone on the side of truth listens to me" (John 18:37). Jesus Christ is the supreme truth teller, and those who want to find the truth must listen to Him.

Writing several hundred years ago, one commentator said that the title "faithful witness" means four things:

1. What God said, Christ made known.
2. He taught without regard to the words of men.
3. He was faithful even in death.
4. He will reveal the truth in the end.

Every man and every woman has to deal with this fundamental issue about Jesus: Can I trust Him? Some people will answer yes, others will say no. Until this issue is settled, there is no point in talking about anything else.

A while back a friend came into my office and said, "You've got to watch 'Donahue' with me." I turned it on, and it was a replay of a broadcast from March 1970. Bob Harrington, the Chaplain of Bourbon Street, and Madalyn Murray O'Hair, the famous atheist, were having a debate. At one point, someone in the audience asked Mrs. O'Hair what she was going to do when Jesus returned. What would she say then? With great confidence, she replied, "It won't happen, so I don't have to worry about that." To which Bob Harrington replied, "The Bible contains 318 verses that speak of the return of Jesus Christ. She's just said He isn't going to return. Over here you've got 318 verses in the book of God, and over there you've got one verse from the book of O'Hair. Now, who you gonna believe?" That's a great question: *Who you gonna believe?* Jesus or Mrs. O'Hair?

My point is this: You have to make the choice for yourself. Who are you going to believe? Let's suppose you don't want to take my word for it. Then read the record for yourself. Let a man take thirty days to read the gospel account with an open mind. Let him read the story for himself and come to his own conclusion. I will tell you what I believe will happen. If that man (or woman) reads with an open mind and an open heart, he or she will come to the inevitable conclusion that what Jesus said is true, that He is the truth, and that His word can be eternally trusted.

I am not saying anything in this chapter to try to prove it to you. I simply challenge you to read the Bible for yourself. Make up your own mind. When you do, you will find that Jesus is entirely trustworthy. Can you trust Him? Yes you can, for He is the faithful witness.

DOES HE HAVE THE POWER TO HELP ME?

There is a second question the people of this generation would like to ask. *If I trust Him, does He have the power to help me?* The answer is found in John's second title for Jesus Christ. He calls him "the firstborn from the dead." This is a reference to Christ's resurrection from the dead. When He rose from the dead, He was the "firstborn from the dead." What exactly does that mean? It means that He is the first person who ever rose from the dead never to die again.

There are several others Jesus raised from the dead, including Lazarus, who had been dead four days. Each occasion was a remarkable miracle, but they had this in common: All of the people Jesus raised would eventually die again. But not Jesus Himself. When He came forth from the tomb on Easter Sunday morning, He rose once and for all. When He left the grave, He left for good. Therefore, Jesus is the firstborn from the dead in the sense that He is the first in a long line of people who will be raised from the dead never to die again.

I find great comfort in this. One of the hardest things I ever do as a pastor is to preside over the funeral of someone I know. I've done it many times, and I'll do it many more times before it's all over. I know what it's like to stand at the graveside and try to say something hopeful in the cold face of death. It's not easy to pray when someone you love has been taken from you. No wonder the Bible calls death "the last enemy" (1 Corinthians 15:26).

In those moments, I find strength in one thing—and one thing only. Jesus has conquered the grave and done what no mortal man has ever done. He has come back from the dead never to die again. And what of those who believe in Him? What happens to them when they die? Thank God, we are not left to wonder about that. God Himself has spoken on that subject. First Thessalonians 4:14 says, "For if we believe that Jesus died and rose again, even so them also which sleep in Jesus will God bring with him" (KJV). *If we believe.* It is as simple and as difficult as that. You will never convince yourself of the resurrection by camping out in a cemetery. If you go to a cemetery and wait for a resurrection, you'll have to wait a long time. After all, the last one occurred some two thousand years ago. But we have the Word of God, which overrides anything we can see with our eyes. Our faith in the resurrection of the dead does not rest in what our eyes can see. No, our faith rests in that act of God whereby he raised Jesus from the dead. If God can do that, He can do anything.

And so, once again, we are invited to make a choice. If you decide to trust Jesus, does He have the power to help you? Yes, He does, for He is the firstborn from the dead.

WILL HE TAKE CARE OF MY FUTURE?

There is a final question Mr. Dufloth would like to ask. "Suppose I do trust Him, and suppose He does have the power to help me, *will Jesus take care of my future?*" The answer comes in John's final title for Jesus Christ. It is breathtaking in its scope. He calls Jesus "the ruler of the kings of the earth." The word for "ruler" is very strong. It means Jesus is the ultimate authority over all the kings of the earth. They are great, but He is greater. They are mighty, but He is mightier. Millions answer to them, but they answer to Him. He is not merely one of the kings. He is ruler over them all.

Who are the rulers of the earth John is talking about? They are political leaders in their various spheres: mayors and councilmen, chairmen and governors, congressmen and senators, presidents and prime ministers, potentates of every variety. They are small-time kings who rule tiny realms and mighty kings who rule vast empires.

Their names are Clinton, Dole, Netanyahu, Hussein, Mubarak, Mandela, Shamir, Yeltsin, Major, Kohl, Peron, Aquino, Arias Sanchez, Perez Rodriguez, Zhao, Kim, Castro,

Assad, Gandhi, Papandreou, Craxi, Mulroney, Mugabe, and Hashimoto. And a million others—big and small.

That list would have to be revised in six months because the leaders of this world come and go, strutting onto the stage of history, playing their part, and then disappearing, only to be remembered as a tiny footnote in some musty book. No leader—no matter how great—stays in power forever. All of them die sooner or later, only to be replaced by some other temporary occupant of the seat of power.

Jesus is ruler over them all. Now it's true this world is in a mess. That's why it's hard to believe this is true. All the evidence seems to move in the opposite direction. The pornographers go free, the baby-killers are untouched, the drug dealers make their millions, the nations arm themselves for total destruction. Indeed, when you look around, you could make a good case that Satan is the ruler of the kings of the earth.

But it will not be that way forever. Satan has no power except that granted to him by God. In due time and at the proper moment, Jesus will step back on the stage of world history. Think of it. The hands that were nailed to the cross will someday rule the world. Though we do not see it today, it is certain and sure of fulfillment. That is what the book of Revelation is all about. Read it for yourself and see how the story comes out.

In the meantime, Jesus is the ruler of the kings of the earth. I admit, it doesn't look that way. I admit, Satan's forces are on the march. I admit, the bad guys seem to be winning. I admit, it's the middle of the fourth quarter and our team is behind by four touchdowns. I admit it all—and yet it is still true that Jesus is the ruler of the kings of the earth.

So we come to answer the ultimate question. And I don't blame the men of this generation for pausing before they answer. Can I trust Him? If I trust Him, does He have the power to help me? If He has the power to help me, will

He take care of my future? That is, not for today alone, but also for tomorrow and for eternity?

Yes, He will, for He is the ruler of the kings of the earth. You're in good hands when you are in His hands, for those hands rule the universe.

WE'D HAVE A PROBLEM THEN, WOULDN'T WE?

Not long ago I had breakfast with an atheist. It turned out to be a most enlightening experience. Although we were meeting for the first time, I immediately came to appreciate his many positive qualities. He was charming, friendly, positive, talkative, and obviously very well educated. He was raised Catholic and had attended a Catholic high school and two excellent Catholic universities. Sometime during his college years, he abandoned not only the Christian faith but his belief in God. He actually converted from Christianity to atheism. He truly believes there is no God.

As we talked, he kept emphasizing that only this life has meaning. Since there is no life after death, what we do now becomes vitally important. Heaven for him is just a myth that religious people use to comfort themselves in times of trouble. We had a long talk, and I learned a great deal from him. It's always useful to see yourself as others see you.

I came away from our time together with three fundamental observations:

1. How difficult it is to be an atheist.
2. How hard you must work to keep your "faith."
3. How careful you must be lest you start believing in God.

Toward the end of our time together, I asked him what he thought about Jesus Christ. He seemed a bit surprised by that question, as if it had no relevance to the question of God's existence. It was my turn to be surprised when he told me that he hadn't thought very much about Jesus one way or the other. He then ventured to say that Jesus was probably a great man and a learned teacher—but He probably never meant to start a religion. That happened after He died and His followers wanted to honor His memory.

Upon hearing that, I decided to press the point. What about His resurrection? What if He really did rise from the dead? My friend stopped for a moment, thought a bit, and then a smile crossed his face. "Well, we'd have a problem then, wouldn't we?" Exactly! If Jesus really did rise from the dead, then He really is the Son of God and God really does exist.

Jesus is the best proof of God's existence. In our witnessing we should bring people back again and again to Jesus Christ. He is the ultimate argument for God because He was in fact God in human flesh. "In the beginning was the Word, and Word was with God, and the Word was God. . . . The Word became flesh and made his dwelling among us" (John 1:1, 14).

BILL'S STORY

A businessman named Bill grew up in a home hostile to the very idea of God's existence. His mother told him, "I don't care if you become a drug addict or a bank robber or if you bring home a boyfriend instead of a girlfriend. There's just one thing I don't want you to do in life—become a Christian." So Bill adopted a lifestyle consistent with his atheism. He lived a life of sexual conquest and suffered the consequences of broken marriages and destroyed relationships. He drank heavily, used drugs, and became a workaholic.

One day Bill looked at his life and cried out to the God he had rejected. "Please get me out of this mess!" He went to an all-night bookstore, and underneath a pile of pornographic magazines found a Bible! All his life he had criticized it but had never read it. That very night he began to read it. The more he read, the more he was convinced that Jesus was and is who He claimed to be. Suddenly it hit him. It's true. There is a God, and Jesus Christ is His Son. After three decades of the hollowness of atheism, he admitted his sin and asked Jesus to save him.

Jesus changed Bill's life radically. He broke free from alcohol and drugs and rebuilt his life. He began to share Christ with others. He even learned to love his mother, who still hated God.

Bill's full name is William J. Murray. He is Madalyn Murray O'Hair's oldest son. His autobiography is called *My Life Without God*. It tells how an atheist found God through a personal relationship with Jesus Christ.

GRIP FAST TO JESUS CHRIST

What's the application? *Hold fast to Jesus Christ. There is no security anywhere else.* It is an eternal fact that today as yesterday, and tomorrow as today, He is the answer to the deepest questions of life.

And so we come to the end of this chapter. I think of Tom Dufloth and of millions just like him. Good and decent, struggling to keep his family together, he passes from one day to the next doing the best he can. What is it that he would like to know about Jesus Christ? There are three questions that sum it up.

- *Can I trust Him?* Yes, I can, for He is the faithful witness.
- *Does He have the power to help me?* Yes, He does, for He is the firstborn from the dead.
- *Will He take care of my future?* Yes, He will, for He is the ruler of the kings of the earth.

We all need Him and we need Him more than we know. This truth is worth repeating: You're in good hands when you are in His hands, for those hands rule the universe. Place your life in His strong hands and you will never be disappointed.

10

HOW A GOOD MAN DIES

F ear not that your life shall come to an end, but rather that it shall never have a beginning." These words by John Henry Newman call us to keep our lives in perspective and to remember what is truly important.

All of us are planning to live a long time, but these days you can never be sure. The stray bullet, the out-of-control driver, the renegade gang member, or the sudden heart attack—who knows? Any one of us could be struck down at any moment.

Suppose you knew you were going to die in the next twenty-four hours? What would you do? Where would you go? And what would you say to the people you love?

Perhaps you are in the hospital dying of some dread disease. You know the end is near. As you search for the right things to share, a thousand thoughts flood your mind. What can you say in your dying moments that will sum up your life? How do you compress sixty or seventy or eighty years of living into just a few sentences?

But what if you don't have three minutes? What if you're involved in a terrible accident while traveling on the interstate? What if you have only thirty seconds? What would you say to your loved ones?

Or suppose you are in the hospital and your loved ones are gathered around you waiting to hear your last words. What would you say?

It's one of those questions that's always theoretical—until the moment comes and you really have only thirty seconds to live. Before that, it's a question you kick around with some friends late at night over a cup of coffee.

A few months ago I thought about this, and I decided that if I had only thirty seconds to live, I would gather my boys around me and tell them four things:

1. Take care of your mother.
2. Love each other.
3. Marry a Christian girl.
4. Serve Jesus Christ forever.

That's it. Thirty seconds and I would be gone. Those four statements summarize everything I would want my boys to know. After that, I would be ready to go.

Not Many Deathbed Scenes

The Bible is a book of life, and so it is no surprise to us that only a few deathbed scenes are recorded. The Old Testament generally tells us that so-and-so lived so many years and then died. We generally don't know when or where or how death took place, so in most cases we don't know about any last words that may have been spoken. We don't know if he gave a thirty-second (or three-minute) summation before his death.

In the New Testament we have even less information. We are not told how most of the chief characters—including the great apostle Paul—died. That's understandable, for the gospel is a message about life. The writers weren't interested in telling how people died. We know how Jesus died, and Judas, and Stephen, and one or two others, but that's about it. The New Testament says very little about death and a great deal about life.

In light of that it is fascinating to note how much space is given in the book of Genesis to the death of Jacob. Abraham's death is described in seven verses (25:5–11), Isaac's in three verses (35:27–29) and Joseph's in five verses (50:22–26). By contrast Jacob's death covers some seventy-three verses. The story begins at the end of chapter 47, covers all of chapters 48 and 49, and closes in the first half of chapter 50.

Jacob's death is recorded in four scenes. First, he meets with Joseph and makes him promise to bury him in the Promised Land (47:28–31). Second, Jacob blesses the two sons of Joseph—Ephraim and Manasseh (48). Third, he blesses his children (49:1–28). Fourth, he again asks to be buried in the Promised Land, and then he dies (49:29–50:14). Each of these scenes reveals something important about how a good man dies.

It is a beautiful and moving story, and one cannot help thinking, *That's the way I would like to die someday—having lived many years, still in my right mind, full of faith in God, and with my family gathered around me.* Our circumstances may conspire to make that impossible, but we can all have the same faith when we die that Jacob had.

Scene # 1: Jacob and Joseph (Genesis 47:28–31)

Jacob is an old man now, 147 years old, and the long years have taken their toll on his body. He barely stands now, tottering uncertainly, leaning for support on the top of his staff. He knows full well that he has an appointment with death. The Bible says, "It is appointed unto man once to die, but after this the judgment" (Hebrews 9:27 KJV).

Death is inevitable. It is the one appointment you must keep. Many of us would rather not face this fact, but it is true. I remember the first time the thought of my own death gripped me. It happened in the days leading up to my thirtieth birthday. Until then I truly never thought for even a moment about my own death. But all that changed as I contemplated the beginning of a new decade. No longer could I kid myself that I was a teenager who would probably live forever. Something inside me said, *You're going to die someday.* That thought terrified me, haunted me, kept me awake at night for weeks as I approached my birthday.

It wasn't that I expected to die *then*, as if some strange accident would cut me down and leave my wife a widow, though I certainly knew that could happen because I had seen it happen to other people my age. No, that wasn't the problem at all.

It was the stark fact that someday—whether sooner or later I did not know—my body would rest in a box six feet underground with a marble marker nestled in the grass saying "Ray Pritchard, 1952–   ." That bothered me tremendously.

George Lawson wrote these words:

> Today we are twenty-four hours nearer to our latter end than yesterday, and three hundred and sixty-five days nearer to it than we were a year ago. At all times we are inexcusable who are warned by the decay of their strength that death is approaching, if they banish it from their thoughts, when they ought to be hastening their preparations to meet it with firmness.[1]

Jacob was not afraid to die. He saw the moment coming and made preparations for his own burial. He had only one request to make of his son Joseph: "Don't bury me in Egypt, but bury me with my fathers." What did that mean? Was it simply a sentimental request to be buried alongside his father and grandfather?

"Dad, Where Do You Want to Be Buried?"

Several years ago, on the first day of a family vacation, we made our way south from Chicago, heading down to Mississippi and on to Florida. Our first day on the road we were having a great time, singing, laughing, and telling jokes. We stopped for lunch in southern Illinois, got back in the car, told more jokes, and laughed some more. Then, out of the blue, our resident theologian, Mark (who was then ten years old), suddenly asked me, "Dad, when you die, where do you want to be buried?"

Talk about a conversation stopper. How do you answer a question like that? After a few moments' thought, I replied, "In the ground." But Mark was serious, so we discussed the question more thoroughly. It was important to Mark to know the answer.

Jacob likewise gave his son Joseph very specific instructions: "Don't leave me in Egypt. Bury me in the Promised Land with my father and my grandfather." This was a wonderful statement of Jacob's faith in God. Two generations earlier God had promised to give the land of Canaan to Abraham and his descendants. In faith Abraham believed God and settled there. In faith Isaac believed God and lived there. Now Jacob is dying in a foreign land. But he believes that someday—though he would not live to see it—his people, his family, his descendants will return to possess the Promised Land. Hebrews 11:9 makes the point that Abraham, Isaac, and Jacob all lived in tents in Canaan, "like . . . stranger[s] in a foreign country." God had promised them the land, but they never took full possession themselves. That would not come for hundreds of years, not until Joshua led the nation of Israel in a victorious campaign of conquest.

The Promises of God Live On

Jacob lived and died without ever knowing of the mighty deeds of Moses and Joshua, for they lived centuries after he. But in Jacob's old age, God gave him faith to believe that although he was dying in Egypt, his future belonged in the Promised Land.

Jacob was saying, "I may be dying, but I believe that one day God will keep His promises. I want to be there when it happens, so don't leave me down here in Egypt. Bury me in the Promised Land." It was his way of saying, "My burial place will be a testimony that God's promises are still true."

That's a great thought, isn't it? Someone has said, "Nothing of God dies when a man of God dies." We die, but the promises of God live on. We are buried, but the promises of God are not buried. Our deaths cannot nullify God's faithfulness.

SCENE # 2: JACOB AND HIS GRANDCHILDREN (GENESIS 48)

The moment of his death is now upon him. With all his strength he rallies one last time and sits up on his deathbed. There he sees Joseph and his two sons, Manasseh and Ephraim. What follows is a touching scene as Jacob says to Joseph, "I never expected to see your face again, and now God has allowed me to see your children too" (v. 11).

Remembering My Grandfathers

I cannot read this passage without thinking about what it means to me personally. I have only a few memories of my grandfathers. Vague memories fill my mind of seeing my father's father—Papa Pritchard—on his farm in Mississippi. He chewed tobacco and had unruly hair and wore work clothes. I remember seeing him at a hospital in Memphis just before he died, when I was still very young.

My mother's father—Grandpa Poduska—lived well into his eighties. Twice we traveled from Alabama to Marshalltown, Iowa, to see him and Grandma Poduska. He was short and heavyset, and in our grainy home movies there are pictures of us sitting on his lap, laughing and playing and pulling on his pants leg.

In 1974 my father died just a few weeks after my wife and I were married. The hardest moment for me came as we drove back from Birmingham to Dallas. When we crossed the Alabama state line I began to cry and couldn't stop. For years I had carried a secret deep in my heart—so deep I had never shared it with anyone. My dream was to someday have a son and name him after my father, whose name was Tyrus Raymond Pritchard. Tears rolled down my face as I realized my daddy would never see his grandchildren. Five years later our first child was born. We named him Joshua Tyrus Pritchard after the grandfather he never knew. To this day there is deep pain in my heart because my father never knew his grandchildren and my boys never knew their grandfather.

The Younger over the Older—Again!

So I understand what it meant when Jacob said, "I never expected to see your face again, and now God has allowed me to see your children too." But now there was more than just seeing the grandchildren. Jacob was to bless the two boys. According to the custom of the time, the primary blessing should have gone to the older son—Manasseh. But that's not how it worked out. When Joseph brought the two boys forward, he put Manasseh in front of Jacob's right hand and Ephraim in front of his left hand. But Jacob crossed his arms, placing his right hand on Ephraim and his left hand on Manasseh. Thus the younger son got the primary blessing and the older son got the lesser blessing.

On one level this is the sovereignty of God at work. He had chosen Ephraim over Manasseh, and although Joseph protested, he could not change the plan of God. On another level, Jacob the younger son was following a pattern of his life. He, the younger, had been chosen over Esau the older. Later on he preferred the younger Rachel to the older Leah. Now he blessed the younger over the older.

Some of us who are younger sons and daughters can draw great encouragement from this story. Many times the firstborn children are favored and children that come later are overlooked. But the Bible is full of hope for younger children. Isaac was a younger child. So was Jacob. So was Joseph. So was Moses. So was Gideon. So was David.

In blessing the younger over the older, Jacob teaches us that God is no respecter of persons. He exalts those who honor Him, regardless of their background or birth order. Very often it is through the "overlooked" people of the world that God does His greatest work.

SCENE # 3: JACOB AND HIS CHILDREN (GENESIS 49:1–28)

Then Jacob asked his sons to gather around him for one final farewell. Beginning with Reuben, the firstborn, he pronounced a blessing or prophecy upon each son individually. The words were crucial, for they described not only what would happen to each son but to the tribes that would eventually come forth from them. Verse 28 explains it this way: "All these are the twelve tribes of Israel, and this is what their father said to them when he blessed them, giving each the blessing *appropriate to him*" (italics added). That last phrase grabs our attention. After all those years Jacob knew his sons inside and out—knew their weaknesses, their habits, their tendencies, and their ambitions. With all that in mind, and speaking under the inspiration of the Holy Spirit, he pronounced a blessing on each son. Some are striking:

> Reuben, who sinned, will lose his place of leadership.
> Simeon and Levi will be dispersed throughout Israel.
> Judah will bring forth the Messiah.
> Zebulun will dwell along the seashore.
> Asher will produce crops for kings.

And on it went, each son receiving a blessing or prophecy perfectly suited to him. Hundreds of years later the tribes would emerge, still bearing the personality traits of their founders.

At first glance Genesis 49 may seem far removed from our situation today. After all, it contains nothing but the blessings Jacob gave his sons on his deathbed. We may think it has no interest for us, except perhaps as a historical curiosity or an example of an ancient custom.

But that is not necessarily the case. Several years ago I read a wonderful book called *The Blessing*, by Gary Smalley and John Trent. Their thesis is that parents have a holy obligation to pass on a blessing to their children. They point out that children who don't receive a blessing from their parents go through life trying to find that sense of approval and self-worth in other places. Some turn to alcohol and drugs, others to a workaholic lifestyle. Still others go through a series of failed relationships, but always they are looking for the affirmation they never received at home.

> If you are a parent, learning about the family blessing can help you provide your child or children with a protective tool. The best defense against a child's longing for imaginary acceptance is to provide him with genuine acceptance. By providing a child with genuine acceptance and affirmation at home, you can greatly reduce the likelihood that he or she will seek acceptance in the arms of a cult member or with someone in an immoral relationship. Genuine acceptance radiates from the concept of the blessing.[2]

Where do you think these authors got the biblical basis for the family blessing? They got it from the life of Jacob—from the blessing he received from Isaac and the blessings he gave to his sons.

According to Smalley and Trent, blessing another person involves five key elements:

- Meaningful touch.
- A spoken message.

- Attaching "high value" to the one being blessed.
- Picturing a special future for the one being blessed.
- An active commitment to fulfill the blessing.

As you study Genesis 48–49, it is clear that Jacob is doing all those things for his sons and grandsons. He is thus fulfilling his ultimate responsibility—blessing his family in the name of the Lord. What a positive example Jacob is for all of us today. Let us go and do likewise for our loved ones.

SCENE # 4: JACOB DIES (GENESIS 49:29–50:14)

The story now comes rapidly to a close. When Jacob had finished blessing his sons, he once again requested to be buried in the Promised Land. Clearly, this was no small issue to him. In one sense it didn't matter where he was buried, for he belonged to God regardless of where his body was laid to rest. But for him the issue was bigger than that. He wanted his burial place to be a testimony to the fact that he never stopped believing in God.

Earlier, when Jacob had first asked to be buried in the Promised Land, Joseph swore to do that, and then Genesis 47:31 added this phrase: "And Israel worshiped as he leaned on the top of his staff." That is, Jacob praised God as he was dying. Interestingly, that is what Jacob is praised for in the book of Hebrews. When the writer considers all Jacob's deeds over his long life, the writer singles out this one event and says of him, "By faith Jacob, when he was dying, blessed each of Joseph's sons, and worshiped as he leaned on the top of his staff" (Hebrews 11:21).

It is always good to praise God, but it is especially meaningful to stand at the end of a long life and say, "God has been good to me." That is a great testimony. It is one of the chief benefits of old age.

Psalm 92:12-15 says that the righteous are blessed with long life and good health and fruitfulness even into old age.

156

They don't dry up and wither away, but they stay fresh until the end.

But note how the righteous end their lives. They leave this world praising God all the way. With the psalmist they proclaim, "The Lord is upright; he is my Rock, and there is no wickedness in him" (92:15). Only those who have seen life in all its fullness can say that with conviction. Here is a fundamental difference between the old and the young. The young know the words to the song; the old know the composer.

A MESSAGE FOR OLDER MEN AND WOMEN

The really important lessons of life are learned only through hard experience. Only those who have known suffering and hardship can say with deep conviction, "The Lord is upright. All that He does is good. He makes no mistakes—and He made no mistakes in my life." It is only looking back that the testimony of the righteous is seen in its full power.

Some blessings are given to the young—to marry, give birth, and raise a family; to set out to conquer the world; to find a mountain and climb it; to raise children for the glory of God; to have a career, to rise in one's profession, to make a mark with one's life. Those things occupy the early decades of adult life.

But the old have a different calling. They have already completed the tasks of early adulthood, having persevered through years of struggle and long nights of prayer, seeing their children grow up, go off to school, find mates, get married, and get started in life. They have seen their children and their grandchildren, and perhaps even their great-grandchildren. Some of them have lived so long that they have outlived their friends. Perhaps they have buried a husband or wife along the way.

To the old is given in the sunset years a privilege that only comes to those who last that long. At the age of forty-four I can only testify to my life so far. But older men have lived far longer, and they know from experience things I have not yet discovered.

FRED STETTLER

In 1923 a young man traveled from Switzerland to America to study at the Moody Bible Institute in Chicago. When he arrived he barely spoke any English. Somehow he found his way to an eight-year-old church in suburban Oak Park. When he needed a place to stay, the people in the little church offered to let him sleep in a closet in the balcony. That's where he lived until he graduated in 1925. And so began a seventy-year association of Fred Stettler and the church I pastor, Calvary Memorial Church.

In January of 1926 he left for the mission field. After spending a year in Romania, he moved to Poland. From 1927 to 1939 he was in a "great and blessed work" of preaching the gospel in that land. With the winds of war sweeping across Europe, Fred Stettler moved from Poland into Switzerland, where he worked with the Open Brethren for some six or seven years. As soon as the war was over, he ministered to the millions of homeless people. That relief work continued for a number of years. In the early fifties he started a ministry he always regarded as the crowning work of his life, the work of literature distribution. From a small center in Switzerland he and his coworkers sent gospel literature in twenty-five different languages to forty countries around the world, never charging a cent, raising the money by faith, sending material out by the ton.

When Fred Stettler died on October 26, 1993, he was ninety-one years old. He had retired from his missionary ministry four months before, having served on the mission field for sixty-seven years. For sixty-seven years our church supported him through the Roaring Twenties, the Great Depression, World War II, the Marshall Plan, the Korean War, the Vietnam War, and on up to the nineties.

I never met him personally, for he spent his last twenty-eight years in Europe without returning to America. What makes a man continue in the work of the Lord for sixty-seven years? Why didn't he retire and go fishing? On his eighty-fifth birthday he wrote a letter to the church that provides part of the answer.

> Yes, my eighty-fifth birthday has passed. A number of congratulations from dear friends have come, and my own family has in mind to have a gathering of the family as soon as all are free to attend. The word of Psalm 23, "He leadeth me in the paths of righteousness for his name's sake," has been a dominant note through all my life. And the word given me when I left for the mission field in 1926 by Miss Martha Grosser was, "He shall bring it to pass," and "commit thy way unto the Lord." The Lord has done great things for me and my family and unto the ends of the world.

There, I think, is the answer—the secret of a life of remarkable effectiveness for God. He went to the mission field with our prayers and one verse of Scripture—"Commit thy way unto the Lord; trust also in him; and he will bring it to pass" (Psalm 37:5 KJV). If there is a secret, that's it. He went overseas in 1926 with one verse of scripture, and sixty-seven years later he entered heaven with a testimony to the very end that God had been faithful to him.

Not long before he died he sent out this message to his friends:

> Being now 90 years and 5 months old my health has not been too well. My mind is no more as it used to be. Weakness in a physical way makes me cancel invitations and next Sunday might be one of the last services I shall hold in public. But during 60–70 years I was blessed a hundredfold by His enablement. Thus I have much to praise the Lord. I have now one great obligation to devote much time in prayer and thank the Lord for all the years of His enabling.

When I read that, I say to myself, *Fred Stettler is a great man, and he serves a great God.*

THROUGH THE DARK VALLEY

"Even though I walk through the valley of the shadow of death, I will fear no evil, for you are with me; your rod and your staff, they comfort me" (Psalm 23:4). The paths of the shepherd lead to the dark valleys eventually. We can't stay in the sunlight forever. Dark valleys are as much a part of our experience as the green pastures or the quiet waters.

Dark valleys—here is where the skill of the shepherd is seen. Can he keep his flock together? Will all of them make it safely through? Will any be lost or harmed?

The Best Part of the Twenty-third Psalm

The best two words in Psalm 23 are two little words in verse 4: "You are *with me.*" The shepherd is no longer up ahead leading the flock. The valley is too dark for that. Now He is walking with us, step-by-step, side-by-side, reassuring His sheep by His calm presence.

If God is with us, we have nothing to fear.

Death casts a frightening shadow over all of life. Visit any hospital or nursing home and you will see the fear on the faces of the patients. Go to a funeral and watch the faces of the mourners. One reason we hate funerals is because we don't want to face the truth of our own mortality.

We can struggle with many other enemies, but we can't struggle with death. The grim reaper wins every time.

We will all eventually go through the valley of the shadow of death. We need a guide to help us find our way through that land of darkness to the light on the other side. Where will we find a guide who can take us through that valley? We've got to find someone who's been there before, who's gone through himself, who can take us by the hand and lead us where he's already been.

The Guide We Need

Whom can we get? Where can we find a guide like that? His name is Jesus! He's been there before. He knows the way through. He's been to the light on the other side—and He'll come for us.

Thanks be to God, we don't walk through that valley alone. Jesus will walk with us. He'll lead us through to the other side.

Deep in my soul, I believe that the saints of God have nothing to fear in the moment of death. Though it may not be pleasant or painless, though it come after long suffering or in a fiery crash, the moment itself will be filled with joy, as the Lord Himself escorts God's children through the darkest valley of all. At that moment, all other guides must turn back. Only the Lord Jesus Christ can help us through. And He does.

NOTES

1. George Lawson, *Lectures in the History of Joseph*, quoted in James Montgomery Boice, *Genesis: An Expositional Commentary*, vol. 3 (Grand Rapids: Zondervan, 1995), 242.
2. John Smalley and John Trent, *The Blessing: Giving and Gaining Family Approval* (Nashville: Nelson, 1986), 18.

11

WHY GOD DRIES OUR TEARS

The call came at about 10:30 P.M. Someone had died. Would I please call the family? Before I could pick up the phone, the mother had called me. Her son had taken drugs and had died earlier that evening at St. Francis Hospital. As I got dressed to go to the home, I wondered what I would say. When I got there everyone was milling around in a state of confusion. At length, the mother took me aside and through her tears asked me the inevitable question, the question I had known was coming. Why? Why did God let this happen to my son?

It was not the first time I have had no satisfactory answer to that question, and unfortunately it won't be the last. For when you look at the questions of life and death, and when you consider the problems of this death-sentenced generation, even the most fervent believer looks up to the heavens and cries out, Why? Why me? Why now? Why this?

PAT NIXON

By all accounts Pat Nixon—former First Lady and the wife of President Richard Nixon—was a wonderful, gracious lady. At her funeral Billy Graham said, "In all my life, and I've known the Nixons for forty years, I never heard a single person say a single negative thing about Pat Nixon." That's a great thing to have said about you. When the service ended an honor guard carried the casket away while the choir sang "America the Beautiful." At that moment the camera zoomed in on President Nixon, once the most powerful man in the world. As they took his wife's casket away, he reached up with his hand and brushed his tears away.

What a lesson there is for us. It doesn't matter whether you're rich or poor. It doesn't matter whether you were the president of the United States or the humblest worker in the country. If you live long enough, you will know pain. You will know heartache. You will brush the tears away as death comes to your door.

Why? The question rings across the centuries and through every generation. All of us ask it sooner or later. If you haven't yet, you will.

It's a question that does not admit of an easy answer. Indeed, the most godly believers have sometimes wondered about the ways of God. And if Job never got an answer, what can I expect? As I read the Bible, I don't think there is one single answer to that question.

But there are answers. And men and women of faith have found them true throughout the centuries.

AN UNEXPECTED ANSWER

One answer tucked away in the Bible may surprise you. It is found in a New Testament book we don't read very much: Second Corinthians. There, in the first verses of the first chapter, you will find a perspective on the heartaches of life that may help you.

When tragedy strikes, most of us look over our shoulders, peer into the past, and search through days gone by to see if we can't find some unconfessed sin or the record of a kindness left undone. We search for a glaring misdeed that will explain why misfortune has come our way. Perhaps, we think, some unconfessed sin will rise up to greet us and we will have our answer. "Aha!" we say, "We deserved this tragedy."

The temptation to do that is almost irresistible, but that approach almost always leaves us confused and frustrated. Who can total up the record of his life and be sure he has counted everything accurately?

Second Corinthians 1:3–7 gives another approach to the reason trials and troubles come to us: Some things happen to us, so that when we are comforted by God, we are then able to comfort someone else. The issue is not necessarily in the trial itself, but in how we respond and what we do after the trial is over. *God comforts you so that you might comfort others.*

THE GREAT PRINCIPLE: GOD COMFORTS US (VV. 3–4A)

Verses 3–4a state the great principle: *There is a divine purpose at work in your life and in mine and that divine purpose begins with God.* He is given two different titles in verse 3: "Praise be to the God and Father of our Lord Jesus Christ, *the Father of compassion* and *the God of all comfort*" (italics added).

The Father of Compassion

Dad, do you remember what it was like when your kids got sick? They had a tummy ache or a headache or were cranky, and you would say to your wife, "Honey, take care of them." And your wife would do what she could, and finally the time would come to put the kids in bed and they would still be whining and crying.

That happened many times with all three of our boys, especially when our oldest son, Joshua, was very young. We would put Joshua in his crib, and then my wife would go to bed exhausted from the cares of the day. About thirty minutes later Joshua would begin to cry. Like a good father, I would roll over in bed and put the pillow over my head, hoping that the noise would go away or that my wife would get up. Eventually I would go to Joshua's room and pick him up. I would put him over my shoulder and walk around the house, singing, "Good little boys don't cry, cry, cry. Good little boys don't cry, cry, cry. Good little boys don't cry, cry, cry, 'cause it makes their daddy mad." We would walk back and forth through the night. I did this many times. After thirty or forty-five minutes of my singing and walking, Joshua would finally fall asleep. I would put him back to bed and go back to bed myself.

Now I'm not a perfect father, but I would do that for my son. Would God do any less for me? No, he would do far more. He is a Father of Compassion.

The God of All Comfort

There is a second title He is given in verse 3. He is called the God of all comfort. The Greek word for comfort comes from a term that means to come alongside someone and help him out. A poor fellow walks down the road, stooped over and with a heavy load on his back. He is tired and weary, and it is hot. You watch him bending lower and lower, and you think, *If I don't help this poor man, he is going to fall.* So you come over, take the load off his back, put it on your back, and you help him carry it.

That's what it means to comfort someone in the biblical sense. You see him carrying a heavy load, and you take it and put it on your own back. Paul is telling us that God is like that. He sees us in our burdens and difficulties and hard times, and He, the God of the Universe, comes and takes the load from us and carries it Himself.

Not only that, but when God does it, He does it all the time. Notice what verse 4 says: "Who comforts us in *all* our troubles" (italics added). That means that when I am sick, He is there by my bedside. When I run out of money, He is there with me in my poverty. When I am hated and despised,

He is with me outside the camp. And when I walk through the valley of the shadow of death, He takes me by the hand and He leads me on through.

A GREAT MISSIONARY PURPOSE: THAT WE MIGHT COMFORT OTHERS (V. 4B)

That much we already know. But there is something you may not know. It's a wonderful perspective on the trials of life. The second part of verse 4 tells us that there is a great purpose at work in the comfort we receive from God. He "comforts us in all our troubles, *so that we can comfort those in any trouble with the comfort we ourselves have received from God*" (italics added). What an insight! There is great missionary purpose in the tragedies of life. God is at work in an unusual way in the hardships of our lives. He allows some things to come to us to soften our hearts so that we might have compassion for those in difficulty and come alongside them and lift their burdens.

It Was God's Will

A number of years ago, I attended a large Christian college in the southeast. It was founded by a dynamic preacher who had built it up over the years into a thriving institution of several thousand students. The heartbeat of the school was the church that was associated with it. Every Sunday morning and every Sunday evening the founder of the school would preach great messages. He was a pulpit giant, and it is also fair to say that he was a very strong man. You didn't want to cross him because he didn't suffer fools gladly.

Then one day he lost his voice. That's the worst thing that can happen to a preacher. This man had built the school on his preaching ministry. He didn't know what he was going to do. He lost his voice so completely that he could barely get up and address the congregation. He traveled across America trying to get his voice back. Finally, he went to a clinic where they performed an operation that solved the problem. Soon after this dynamic leader resumed his ministry, I talked to a man who had known him for over a quarter of a century. He made a comment I have never forgotten. It was God's will that he lose his voice. For many years he had a hard time understanding people who weren't as strong and energetic as he. He tended to be hard on people with weaknesses. Now there is a new note of compassion in his ministry.

A Softer Heart

That is exactly what the apostle Paul is talking about. *Our afflictions soften our hearts so that when we have received the comfort of God, it is easy for us to pass it along to someone else.* Oh, how we need this in the church of Jesus Christ. It is so easy to be callous. It is so convenient to be unkind. It is so easy to look down our noses at weaker brothers and sisters who go through hard times. We say so carelessly, "Why don't they just get tough? Why don't they show some backbone? Why don't they quit complaining and get on with life? Why can't they be strong like the rest of us?" The apostle Paul is telling us that one of the reasons God lets us go through hard times is to break us of that attitude and soften us up so that we are able to minister in the name of Jesus Christ to other hurting people.

This is a mighty principle that answers many questions. Many of us have hardened places in our lives that will not become tender until we go through the fires of affliction. God lets that happen so that we might reach out to others and comfort them.

THE GREAT PROVISION: CHRIST'S OVERFLOWING COMFORT (V. 5)

Verse 5 gives us the great provision that makes this sharing of comfort possible. Paul says, "For just as the sufferings of Christ flow over into our lives, *so also through Christ our comfort overflows*" (italics added). Paul is not implying that we somehow share in the vicarious sufferings of Jesus Christ, as if the work of Jesus Christ on the cross were not enough. Nor is he saying that just as Jesus died for the sins of the world so, too, we can die for the sins of others. No, he's not talking about that at all.

We Are Not Exempt from His Sufferings

When Jesus was on the earth He didn't walk an easy road. He knew suffering and privation and hardship and discouragement and opposition and persecution. Paul is saying that those who follow the Lord Jesus Christ will know the same difficulties. They will not be exempt from sickness and hardship and suffering and all of the things that are part of what it means to be a follower of Jesus Christ. Those who believe in Jesus Christ share in His sufferings. As He suffered on this earth, so also shall we.

When I was a pastor in California, I would come down to the church early on Sunday morning to work on my sermon. Then I would walk throughout the sanctuary, stopping at different pews to pray for people by name. (That was easy, because people always sat in the same place.) I would pray for Carl Hale, who sat on the right about six pews back. Rick and Joanne Hale always sat down front. Gladys Crigler usually sat on my left, and Florence Martini would be near the center aisle. Stan and Jan Quillan would be almost halfway back. I would walk up and down the aisles of my church, stopping to pray where I knew my people would be sitting in just a few hours. Here is the truth: I never got through the whole congregation. Not because there were so many people, but because there were so many problems.

The Wounded Healer

Paul is telling us even more than that. He is telling us that as the suffering overflows, even more so does the comfort. Look back at the verse: "For just as the sufferings of Christ flow over into our lives, so also through Christ our comfort overflows." The phrase *flow over* and the word *overflows* are different forms of the same Greek word. Sufferings overflow. Comfort overflows. The greater the suffering, the greater the comfort. The greater the comfort, the more I have to share with others.

What a thought! My sufferings qualify me to minister to other people. Henri Nouwen has written a book titled *The Wounded Healer*. He meant it, I think, as a description of the pastor, but it applies to every Christian. We are all wounded with the failures of life and the things that weigh us down. And it is to wounded men and women that God has committed the great ministry of healing other people.

The Man from Belgium

An amazing thing happened in Dallas a few years ago. Herman Moody, a forty-seven-year-old import-export specialist, was dying of leukemia. The cancer center at Baylor Hospital told him he had only one chance. He needed a bone marrow transplant. That's all they could do for him now. He was dying of leukemia. They told him it had to be a perfect match. So they took a sample of his bone marrow and put it into a computer system, a worldwide registry of people who have volunteered to donate their bone marrow. They found a match. Only one problem. The man was in Belgium. When the man was contacted, he volunteered to come to America on behalf of a man he had never met. When he arrived, almost a liter of bone marrow was taken from his hip and given to Herman Moody.

A man who is living, gives to save a man who is dying. It's a long way from Belgium to Texas. Why would a man do a thing like that, especially for someone he had never met? His answer went something like this: "Several years ago my brother died of cancer, and his death broke my heart. After he died I promised God that if I could, I would help someone else stay alive. That's when I signed up with the bone marrow registry."

But that's not the whole story. The man from Belgium added, "When I go to church, I hear the priest talking about loving my neighbor. How could I refuse to help my brother if he is in need? When they called and asked if I would travel to Dallas, as a Christian I could not say no."

That's what Paul is saying. Once we have suffered, we are able to comfort others *out of the overflowing comfort of Jesus Christ.*

THE GREAT EXAMPLE: THE RIPPLE EFFECT (V. 6)

Paul was not content to let the matter rest there. He goes on to offer the example of his own life. He states it quite plainly in verse 6: "If we are distressed, it is for your comfort and salvation; if we are comforted, it is for your comfort, *which produces in you patient endurance of the same sufferings we suffer*" (italics added). On one hand, when he suffered the result was the Corinthians' comfort and salvation. How? He ministered to them the comfort God gave him. On the other hand, when he himself was comforted, the Corinthians learned encouragement from him so that they could patiently endure those same sufferings.

Let's put it another way. Paul undergoes rejection and opposition to the preaching of the gospel. In the midst of his trials, the God of all comfort comes alongside and takes the heavy load off *his* shoulders. And Paul is comforted. The Corinthians see that, and as they suffer the same things, Paul comes alongside and takes the heavy load off *their* shoulders. So instead of quitting under pressure, they develop patient endurance.

Have you ever gone to a pond out in the country and thrown a pebble into the water? What happens? From the point where the pebble enters the water, ripples spread out farther and farther. What started as a ripple from one small pebble soon affects the whole pond.

That's a picture of what God is doing in your life. He is comforting you in your trials *so that you might comfort another who may comfort another who may comfort another.* And the ripple effect spreads out from you to people you may never even meet.

That brings us back to the place where we began—the uncertainties of life, the midnight phone call, the hospital, the funeral home. Back to the place where we ask, Why has this happened?

There is no one answer that can fully contain God's purposes. No human could ever fully comprehend the Almighty. But these verses offer a perspective we need to remember. God is at work in your life in the time of suffering. Among many other things, He is preparing you to minister to others. God dries your tears so that you might do the same for someone else.

WHY SOME CHRISTIANS NEVER HAVE A MINISTRY TO OTHERS

Some believers never discover this truth. They are perpetual gripers when things get difficult. Life is never fair, they always get the short end of the stick, God has singled them out for punishment.

Such people never have a ministry to others because they constantly fight against God's perspective on their trials and remain tough and hardened when they ought to be soft and tender. As a result, they have nothing to pass along to anyone else.

MISSIONARY EYES

May I suggest one simple step of application? Many of us would like a personal ministry, but we don't know where to begin. This passage suggests that *our personal ministry begins as we share with others what God has shared with us.* That means there are people in your life out there who need the help only you can give. Some of them need a word of encouragement—and you are the only one who can give them that word. Some of them are staggering beneath a heavy load— and you are the only one who can lift that burden from their shoulders. Some of them are about to quit—and you are the only one who can keep them in the race. Some of them have been hit with an incredible string of trials—and you are the only one who can help them bear their trials.

Those people are all around you. Your only problem is that you don't see them. Pray that God will give you Missionary Eyes. Those are eyes that see the real needs of the people you meet. Ask God to give you at least one person you can help this week. Pray that God will bring at least one person across your path who needs the help only you can give.

That's a prayer God will answer, for there are folks all around you who are just barely making it. You see them where you work, and you live next door to them. Your children go to school with their children.

They are out there waiting for someone to give them help. And here we are—recipients of the goodness of God. God has helped us for a purpose: that we might take what we have received and share it with those who desperately need it.

Ask God to give you at least one person you can help this week. And then ask Him for Missionary Eyes to make you sensitive to that person.

God dries our tears that we might do the same for someone else.

12

OUR AWESOME GOD

It's not often that a book title tells the whole story. Usually titles are chosen because they are catchy, not because they are informative. But occasionally you stumble on a title that both catches your attention and also tells you exactly what the book is about. A generation ago J. B. Philips wrote a book called *Your God Is Too Small*. The title says it all. So many of us struggle because our God is much smaller than the God of the Bible. We have Him neatly defined and kept in a box of our own making.

If your God is too small, perhaps you need to take another look at the God of the Bible. Over the centuries theologians have used certain words to describe His essence: sovereign, almighty, omnipotent, omniscient, omnipresent, infinite, eternal, and immortal, to mention only a few. But no list of adjectives could ever adequately picture the immensity of God. He is so big that we don't even have the proper words to describe His bigness. He is bigger than our biggest words and grander than our grandest conceptions. Because He is God, no words or thoughts of mortal men and women could ever encompass His greatness. Our best efforts fall so far short of His divine reality that we flatter ourselves to think that we truly understand Him at all.

It is against that backdrop that we must consider the meaning of verses such as "The secret things belong to the Lord our God" (Deuteronomy 29:29) and "As the heavens are higher than the earth, so are my ways higher than your ways and my thoughts than your thoughts" (Isaiah 55:9). Here we are being told that there is a fundamental category difference between God and His creation. His thoughts are "higher" precisely because He is God and we are not.

Therefore, it shouldn't surprise us that God does many things we don't understand. Or that most of our questions about life will go unanswered. Job discovered this when God engaged him in a long series of questions starting with, "Where were you when I laid the earth's foundation?" (Job 38:4) and ending with, "Who dares to open the doors of his mouth, ringed about with his fearsome teeth?" (41:14). The answer to the first question is "not there"; the answer to the second is "not me." And the answer to every question in between is also in the negative. It's as if God were playing a game of Celestial Jeopardy and managed to sweep the board before Job can answer a single question.

In dealing with our deepest struggles it helps to remind ourselves of who God really is. *The greater our view of God, the more strength we will have to face the trials of life.* Similarly, the lower our view of God, the more likely we are to be blown away when tragedy strikes.

With that background, let's take a look at Romans 11:33–36. Of all the passages in the Bible that speak to God's greatness, perhaps none other contains so much truth compacted into only four verses. No Bible expositor ever feels adequate when faced with a marvelous paragraph like this. It contains depths of truth no one can hope to fully explore, much less to understand. For our purposes we may arrange the major thoughts of these four verses around three sets of three statements each.

First of all, these verses teach us . . .

THREE FACTS ABOUT GOD

He Knows Everything There Is to Know

"Oh, the depth of the riches of the wisdom and knowledge of God!" (v. 33). The apostle Paul was as well acquainted with God as any man ever was, yet he confessed himself at a loss to know the depth of God. How deep is God? So deep that Paul could only stand at the edge and peer into the deep. Those who know the most must confess how little they actually know. If a man claims an intimate knowledge of God, we must suspect that he knows God no better than he knows himself. For God is deeper than our minds can fathom. Not only is His wisdom and knowledge deeper than we know, it's deeper than we can even imagine. We have no mental category for the depth of God's character. We simply know that it is, and that we know nothing about it except what God has chosen to reveal. Trying to understand God is like trying to empty the ocean with a tiny bucket. Dip your bucket into the water a thousand times and you haven't made a dent in the vast expanse of water. Your bucket is too small, your arms too weak, and the ocean too large, wide, and deep. So it is with God. We can't begin to comprehend the depths of His being.

When I was preaching in Kentucky several years ago, I heard a Southern gospel song on the radio. It went like this: "Has it ever occurred to you that nothing has ever occurred to God?" That sounds odd because things "occur" to us all the time, but it's true: Nothing has ever "occurred" to God. He never wakes up and says, "A great idea just occurred to me." In the first place, He never sleeps and, therefore, never "wakes up." In the second place, all His ideas are great. In the third place, He has always known all the great ideas, all the time, from the beginning of time.

Our text suggests that He knows everything that could ever be known. Not only is His knowledge deep, it is also wide. He knows everything that has ever been, everything that is, and everything that will be. He even knows everything that could have been, or could be, or ever could be. Not only does He know it, but He has known it all from the beginning of time.

Several years ago I came across an article on the prevenient grace of God. The phrase *prevenient grace of God* refers to "the grace that goes before." Here's a working definition: In every situation of life, God is already at work before I get there. He is working creatively, strategically, and redemptively for my good and His glory.

Wow! So many times I limit my thinking to the fact that God's presence goes with me as I move through life. That's true, but it's only part of the story. He's not only with me now, He's already way up the road ahead of me.

Think about it this way. While I am struggling with the problems of today, God is at work providing solutions for the things I am going to face tomorrow. He's already there, working creatively in situations I have yet to face, preparing them for me and me for them.

Or to say it another way, while I'm in Tuesday, He's clearing the road for me on Friday. That's what Proverbs 3:6 means when it promises that He "will make your paths straight."

God is already at work providing solutions for problems I don't even know I have yet!

Are you worried about next week? Forget it. He's already there. What about that crucial meeting next Monday? Don't sweat it. He's already there. What about that surgery your oldest daughter faces in a few days? Fear not. He's already there.

It would be enough if God simply walked with you through the events of life as they happen. But He does much more than that. He goes ahead of you, clearing the way, arranging the details of life so that when you get there, you can have confidence that God has already been there before you.

That's the prevenient grace of God. He goes before His people. He's at work in the future while we live in the present. He can do that because He knows everything there is to know.

He Makes Plans We Can't Understand

"How unsearchable his judgments!" (v. 33) Other translators use the word *inscrutable*, which means "beyond human understanding." Not only does God make plans we don't know about, even if we did know about them, we couldn't understand them. That explains why some things remain unexplainable forever. It's not that God is unwilling to explain, it's that our little minds can't begin to comprehend the infinite purposes of God. John Wesley said it this way: "Show me a worm that fully comprehends a man, and I'll show you a man that can comprehend God." It can't be done.

He Alone Knows Why Everything Happens

"And his paths beyond tracing out!" (v. 33). Matthew Henry has a helpful word about this. The main things God wants us to know are clear and plain. "They are," he said, "like a highway open for all to travel. But the judgments of His hands are dark and mysterious. That road is closed forever to us. We must not pry into the mysteries of God, but rather bow before Him in adoration for things we don't understand." Then Henry added this sentence: "God leaves no footprints behind Him." You cannot tell where the Almighty has been or where He is going. He leaves no track or trail that we can follow.

That means that in life many things will happen that we simply do not understand. Sickness, accidents, violent crimes, sudden financial collapse, divorce, crumbled dreams, cancer, tornadoes, hurricanes, earthquakes, floods, famines, war, broken promises, evil triumphing over good, lost jobs, ruined lives, children dying, others promoted while we are passed over, our ideas stolen and used by others, good works we do that others take credit for. The list is endless—and heart-breaking.

A few years ago Michael Gartner wrote in *USA Today* about the sudden death of his seventeen-year-old adopted son Christopher. "He died on Thursday. He was a healthy, robust boy on Tuesday. He got sick on Wednesday. And he died on Thursday." Then he said, "You would have liked him. Everyone did."

The father and the son were a contrast in appearance. Gartner is five-foot-eight and weighs one hundred sixty pounds. Christopher was close to six-foot-four and weighed some three hundred pounds. "He looked like a cement block with a grin."

He died of a sudden attack of juvenile diabetes. Despite heroic medical efforts and fervent prayers, Christopher was suddenly gone. "It is awful and horrible and sad, and no words can comfort his four grandparents, his brother and sister, his friends, or his parents."

The day after the boy died, a friend called Gartner and said the only thing that helped him get through the terrible tragedy: "If God had come to you 17 years ago and said, 'I'll make you a bargain. I'll give you a beautiful, wonderful, happy, and healthy kid for 17 years, and then I'll take him away,' you would have made that deal in a second."

"And that was the deal. We just didn't know the terms," Michael Gartner said. He's right. That's always the deal. And we never know the terms in advance. God gives us life, health, happiness, our children, our friends, and says, "Enjoy it while you can. Someday I will come back for them." And we never know the terms in advance.

Only God knows why things happen. Most of the time we can only wonder.

Second, this text tells us . . .

THREE THINGS NO ONE CAN DO

Verses 34–35 contain three rhetorical questions, each one expecting a negative answer. They all begin with the same two words: "Who has . . . Who has . . . Who has?" The answer is always the same: "No one . . . No one . . . No one."

No One Can Explain God

"Who has known the mind of the Lord?" (v. 34). Lots of people think they know what God is like, but the only things we know about God are the things He has chosen to reveal to us.

I'm sure you've heard the story of the six blind men who were trying to describe an elephant. The first man felt the tusk and said, "An elephant is sharp, like a spear." The second man touched the elephant's massive side and exclaimed, "No! An elephant is like a wall." The third man stroked the wiggling trunk and concluded that an elephant was most like a snake. The fourth man tried to wrap his arms around one of the elephant's legs. When he couldn't, he said, "He is like a tree." The fifth felt the expanse of the elephant's huge ears and said, "It's easy to see that an elephant is much like a fan." The last man felt the tiny tail and said, "You're all wrong. An elephant is shaped like a rope."

Who was right? They all were. Who was wrong? All of them. We are like those blind men when it comes to knowing God. Who among us can claim to fully understand the infinite and Almighty God of the universe? No one knows enough to fully explain God.

No One Can Counsel God

"Or who has been his counselor?" (v. 34). I love the way Eugene Peterson puts it: Is there "anyone smart enough to tell him what to do?" (TM). God needs no counselor, for He is infinitely wise. In high schools there are trained professionals called guidance counselors. They exist to help students make wise decisions about the future. They gather data from report cards, test scores, and detailed interviews, matching the student's strengths and weaknesses with the available opportunities. Such men and women are indispensable because life is filled with so many possibilities.

But God needs no guidance counselor. Indeed, He is the ultimate Counselor. He guides every being in the universe, but no one guides Him. He counsels all creation, but no one is His counselor. For a mere man to counsel God is like a candle trying to give light to the sun.

An ill-prepared college student was struggling through his final exam in economics. He happened to be taking the test just before Christmas. In desperation he scrawled across the bottom of the paper, "Only God knows the answer to these questions. Merry Christmas!" When he got the paper back, the teacher marked it: "God gets 100. You get 0. Happy New Year!"

No one knows as much as God does, no one can explain God, and no one can be His counselor.

No One Can Accuse God of Unfairness

"Who has ever given to God, that God should repay him?" (v. 35). This question comes from Job 41:11, where God asks Job, "Who has a claim against me that I must pay? Everything under heaven belongs to me." No one can ever say, "God, You owe me something," for the Lord will be no man's debtor. No one can say, "You cheated me," for God cheats no one. No one can say, "I've earned Your favor," for everything this side of hell is mercy and everything this side of heaven is grace.

Finally, this text gives us . . .

THREE REASONS TO PRAISE GOD

It is as if Paul can contain himself no longer. He means to show that God is all in all. Everything comes from Him, everything exists by His power, everything will ultimately answer to Him. James Montgomery Boice calls this verse the secret of a Christian worldview, for it dethrones man and puts God on the throne of the universe. Boice makes his point by asking a trivia question: "What was the last song recorded by the Beatles before they broke up?" Answer: "I, Me, Mine." The Beatles' last song, Boice says, is the first and last song of the unregenerate heart. But the song of the redeemed is Romans 11:36!

He Is the Source of All Things

"For from him" (v. 36). He is the source of all things, which means that all things flow from Him. I saw a wonderful illustration of this truth several years ago when I spent a few days at Camp Nathanael in Emmalena, Kentucky. The camp itself is something of a miracle. A man named Garland Franklin was the first director. In the 1930s he was driving along the dirt road next to Troublesome Creek when the Lord spoke to him and said, "I want you to build a camp there." The land wasn't for sale right then, but Mr. Franklin began praying about it. Several years later the land came up for sale, and Franklin's mission raised the money to buy it. This was, of course, in the heart of the Great Depression when money was scarce everywhere, but nowhere scarcer than in the coal-mining country of eastern Kentucky.

Then in 1936 the mission decided to dig a well on the property. After saving up their money, they found that they only had $75 to pay for the well—the digging, the installation of equipment, and any other associated expenses. When the man came to dig the well, Mr. Franklin asked him where he would like to dig. The man said, "Mr. Franklin, I can see into the ground as far as you can." So Garland Franklin pointed to a spot and said, "Dig right there." So they started to dig and hit water after going down only seventy-five feet (most of the other wells in the area go down at least two hundred feet).

After putting in the pump and the permanent casing, enclosing the wellhead and attaching the pipes, the contractor totaled up his bill and presented it to Mr. Franklin. The exact amount was $74.99. They had one penny left over!

But that's not the end of the story. The well they dug in 1936 is still there and still pumping water. But that's not the most amazing fact. In more than sixty years the well has never run dry. Never. Not even for a moment. "It's like there's an ocean of water under there," Franklin says. Several years ago when a severe drought hit the region, most of the local wells went dry, but not the one at Camp Nathanael. They had so much water they let the local people come and fill their water barrels.

And the well shows no signs of ever running dry. Is that a miracle? Yes, but behind the miracle well stands a miracle-working God who can speak a word and an ocean of water comes gushing up through the ground. He is truly the source of all things.

He Is the Sustainer of All Things

"And through him" (v. 36). Not only do all things flow from Him, but He is the reason for the continued existence of the universe. He alone understands the purpose for everything that He created. One of my favorite stories involves George Washington Carver, the man who discovered 255 different things you could do with the lowly peanut. Down South, Dr. Carver is revered for his years of work at the Tuskegee Institute in my home state of Alabama. Because of him, the South began to move away from a cotton-based economy to one based on other crops. Carver was a devout Christian who had a deep knowledge of God.

When he was asked where he came up with so many uses for the peanut, he told this story. He said that when he was a young man, he went for a walk in the fields, and while he was there, he and the Lord had a conversation. When he asked the Lord to show him why He had created the universe, the Lord said, "Son, that's much too big for you. Ask me for something you can understand." So he tried again: "Lord, show me why you created the world." "Still too big for you. Try again." Carver dropped his eyes to the ground and happened to see some peanuts on the vine. "Lord, could you tell me why you created the peanut?" "That's a good question. Now we've found something you can understand." The Lord showed Dr. Carver the secrets of the peanut, and Carver used what God showed him to change the world.

All things come "through him." All knowledge, all wisdom, everything we have comes "through him." He is the sustainer of all things—even the peanut!

He Is the Supreme Purpose of All Things

"And to him are all things" (v. 36). This is a breathtaking statement because Paul includes "all things" in his exclamation. Nothing is left out, no part of creation excluded. God is the beginning, the middle, and the end of "all things." Everything comes from Him, everything continues by Him, everything finds its ultimate purpose in Him.

I am reminded of Augustine's famous words, "You have made us for yourself, and our hearts are restless until they find rest in you." It's no secret that youth gangs are a growing problem in every major American city. In Chicago there are hundreds of gangs ranging from a handful of teenagers in local neighborhoods to vast organizations encompassing thousands of "street soldiers." Many people consider the gang members beyond the reach of the gospel.

But that is not necessarily true. Recently one of our local newspapers carried a story about Glen and Jane Fitzjerrell and their work with some of the toughest kids in Chicago—the gang members on the West Side. The Fitzjerrells know about the Spanish Cobras, the Latin Kings, Satan's Disciples, and all the rest. The only word for their ministry is "remarkable." The headline read "Gangs vs. God: Couple puts out Christian message."

The article starts with this paragraph:

> "Some people serve the Lord beneath a steeple and bell, we run a rescue shop within a yard of hell." Oak Park residents Glen and Jane Fitzjerrell do indeed work within a yard of hell. It is their mission to serve young men and women doing time in the criminal justice system and to minister to those living in the gang-controlled inner city streets. Glen's work focuses on men in gangs while Jane works primarily with the women, either full-fledged gang members or girlfriends of members. Both spend time on the streets talking to gang members and building relationships and visiting kids locked up for various crimes.

"People are often amazed at how freely we can move among the gangs. The key is, the Lord has a lot of respect on the streets," Jane said. When Glen visits a gang member in jail, he always introduces himself the same way: "I'm Glen Fitzjerrell and I am a man of God. I am here to help you."

Jane adds that "It's rare to find a kid who doesn't believe in God. These kids feel so burdened, so guilty. They see the faces of the people they've hurt. Everyone is against them. They have disappointed their mothers, and their gangs don't visit them anymore. They are hungry for relief."

One by one these street-hardened teenagers are coming to Jesus Christ. How does it happen? It starts when Glen and Jane visit the gang leaders in jail. "We introduce them to the Lord, give them an opportunity to accept the Lord in their lives. We've never had a kid turn us down. They know they need God," Glen explained.

All things are made by Him, and through Him, and for Him. He is the source, the means, and the goal of all creation. No wonder these young men and women are coming to Jesus Christ. Although everyone else may have given up on them,

God will never give up on them—not even for a moment. They were made to know God! Think about it—the Chicago gang members are in the Bible! They are part of the "all things" of Romans 11:36.

To Him Be the Glory Forever!

What is left for us but the words of Paul in verse 36? "To him be the glory forever! Amen." The mysteries of God lead us in one of two directions. Either you give up your faith altogether and become a skeptic or you bow the knee before the God who is too great, too vast, too almighty for you to fully comprehend.

God always leaves us with a choice, doesn't He? You can believe and be saved or you can doubt and be damned. But either way many of your questions will never be fully answered. If you choose to believe, then you are left with these final words: "To him be the glory forever!"

In life and in death—*To Him be the glory forever!*

In joy and in sorrow—*To Him be the glory forever!*

In good days and dark nights—*To Him be the glory forever!*

In sickness and in health—*To Him be the glory forever!*

In your career and in your home—*To Him be the glory forever!*

In your marriage and in your children—*To Him be the glory forever!*

In your prosperity and in your poverty—*To Him be the glory forever!*

In days of peace and in times of war—*To Him be the glory forever!*

In gentle breeze and in gathering storm—*To Him be the glory forever!*

In the classroom and in the boardroom—*To Him be the glory forever!*

In moments of victory and in darkest defeat—*To Him be the glory forever!*

In prayers answered and in prayers unanswered—*To Him be the glory forever!*

In yesterday's tears, today's rejoicing, and tomorrow's adventures—*To Him be the glory forever!*

In heaven and on earth—*To Him be the glory forever!*

Whatever comes, whether tragedy or triumph, in the midst of the years, with the changing of the seasons, when we know enough or nothing at all, when hope is gone and all we have left is God,

To Him alone be the glory! Amen.

13

A GLIMPSE OF HEAVEN

It happened so fast that the Reverend Duane Scott Willis hardly had time to react. He and his wife, Janet, were traveling with six of their children on Interstate 94 near Milwaukee on November 8, 1994, when a piece of metal fell from the truck in front of them, rupturing the gas tank in their van. The resulting explosion ripped a hole through the backseat floor. Within seconds flames engulfed the vehicle, instantly killing five of the children. The sixth, thirteen-year-old Benjamin, died the next day. Both parents suffered severe burns.

The tragedy grabbed national headlines as millions of people watched the Willises struggle with every parent's worst nightmare—the death of a child. But in this case the tragedy was multiplied both by the number of children and the manner of their sudden death.

What do you say in a moment like this? A few days after the accident, Reverend Willis and his wife, both still heavily bandaged from their own burns, met the press to share how their faith had sustained them through such a tragedy. "Janet and I have had to realize that we're not taking a short view of life," Willis said. "We take the long view, and that includes eternal life."

In the months after the accident the Willises talked often about the day their family will be reunited in heaven. Sometimes they wondered about the details. Will the family live together again? How old will the children be? What are they doing in heaven right now?

"The Bible doesn't give us definitives. All I can think is, I'm sure we're going to recognize them. I'm going to see my kids again," Pastor Willis explained. Commenting on the tragedy, a *Chicago Tribune* editorial concluded with these words: "There are only two possible responses to the kind of loss that Duane and Janet Willis suffered last week: utter despair or unquestioning faith. For the Willises, despair was never an option."

Along with many others, I stand in awe of the Willises. In the words of Job 23:10, they have been through the fire and have come forth as gold. Who among us can imagine watching six children burn to death and being utterly helpless to do anything about it? But what would destroy many of us has only made them stronger.

How can that be? I find the answer in one simple sentence: "We take the long view, and that includes eternal life." Duane and Janet Willis believe in heaven, and that has made all the difference.

HOME FOR THE HOLIDAYS

On the night before He was crucified, Jesus uttered these famous words to His disciples:

Do not let your hearts be troubled. Trust in God; trust also in me. In my Father's house are many rooms; if it were not so, I would have told you. I am going there to prepare a place for you. And if I go and prepare a place for you, I will come back and take you to be with me that you also may be where I am. (John 14:1–3)

What is heaven like? It's like going home at Thanksgiving to the house where you grew up. It's like getting out of the car and seeing your mother and father standing at the door with their arms stretched out to greet you. It's the biggest family reunion in history in a place Jesus called "my Father's house." When Eugene Peterson translated John 14:1 he used a charming phrase: "There is plenty of room for you in my Father's home" (TM).

"Plenty of room for you"—that's a wonderful thought. But even more wonderful is the truth that heaven is a pre-pared place.

A brief biblical survey reveals the following facts about heaven. It is:

- God's dwelling place (Psalm 33:13).
- Where Christ is today (Acts 1:11).
- Where Christians go when they die (Philippians 1:21–22).
- The Father's house (John 14:2).
- A city designed and built by God (Hebrews 11:10).
- A better country (Hebrews 11:16).
- Paradise (Luke 23:43).

WRONG IDEAS ABOUT HEAVEN

Heaven has gotten bad press lately. We don't believe in it like we used to. We're too busy making a living to worry about what happens after we die.

Many of us have the wrong idea of heaven. We think it's like that commercial where two middle-aged men tap you on the shoulder in the middle of the street and you ride an esca-lator into the clouds while a choir sings. Or we think it's like a television show where apprentice angels return to the earth to do good deeds and help poor earthlings in trouble. Or more generally, we have a vague idea that heaven is some ethereal, misty realm where we float on clouds all day, plucking harps and polishing our halos.

But the truth is much different. Heaven is a real place filled with real people. The Bible pictures it as a great city filled with all of God's people.

A City Built by God

What does such a city look like? It is a city with:

- No pollution, for the skies are always crystal clear.
- No crime or violence, for no criminals ever enter.
- No greedy politicians, drug pushers, or child molesters.
- No potholes, and no power outages, either.

It is filled with abundant parks, rivers, rolling meadows, and flowing streams. Lining the streets are flowers in constant bloom, fruit trees of every kind, every species of plant life growing free from pestilence and disease.

The gates are made of pearl, the walls of jasper, the streets of gold. Precious stones lie on the ground like playthings—emeralds, rubies, diamonds galore.

On every hand are children laughing, bright conversation, music floating from every direction.

In the city that God builds, there are no tears, nor is there sorrow, regret, or remorse. Bitterness is gone forever, failure is left far behind, suffering is redeemed and rewarded. There are no eyeglasses, no braces, no wheelchairs, no false teeth, no bald heads, no hearing aids, and no nursing homes. There are no hospitals, no paramedics, no CPR. Doctors have to find new jobs, for they aren't needed anymore. Aspirin is gone, accidents are over, cancer has disappeared, heart attacks are banished, and AIDS is a distant memory. In heaven no one grows old and feeble.

A CITY WITHOUT CEMETERIES

There is one other thing you won't find in heaven. There are no cemeteries in the city God builds. Why? Because there are no funerals, for in that glad city no one ever dies.

If you make it to that city, you live forever, never to die again. Either you believe in heaven or you don't. It is either a real place or it isn't.

Oral Roberts's oldest son committed suicide at the age of thirty-eight. He had been on drugs ever since returning from a tour of duty in Vietnam. Writing in his diary, Oral recounted the terrible events of his son's last days. Then he added, "Satan has played his last card. Death is all he can do to my son. Satan is finished now. Thanks be to God, there are no graves dug into the hillsides of heaven."

Do you remember the name Chet Bitterman? He was a Wycliffe missionary in Columbia taken captive by guerrillas in early 1981. He had been held for forty-eight days when his body was found in Bogota with one bullet through his heart. Speaking of it later, his father said, "We have eight children. One is in heaven. Seven are on earth."

To the unbeliever such words seem either sentimental or simply incredible. But to the one who accepts God's Word at face value, they are nothing less than the sober truth. If Jesus Christ can be trusted, then heaven is a real place. If heaven is real, then this life is not the end. There really is a city "with foundations, whose architect and builder is God" (Hebrews 11:10).

A PICTURE OF HEAVEN (REVELATION 21:18)

But what is heaven *really* like? The last two chapters of the Bible, Revelation 21–22, written by the apostle John, present the most comprehensive picture of heaven to be found anywhere in Scripture. No other passage gives such a richly detailed picture of our eternal abode. There we learn of streets of gold, gates of pearl, and city walls studded with emeralds, rubies, and diamonds. We discover who will be in heaven and who won't be there and why. We learn about the river of life and the Tree of Life, with its leaves for the healing of the nations.

A New Heaven and a New Earth

John begins his description with these encouraging words: "I saw a new heaven and a new earth" (21:1). The word *new* in this passage means new in quality. Absolutely, totally new. It suggests fresh life rising from the decay and wreckage of the old world.

What happens to the current earth on which we live? Second Peter 3:10 tells us that a day is coming when "the heavens will disappear with a roar; the elements will be destroyed by fire, and the earth and everything in it will be laid bare." Evidently God will dismantle the entire universe in a great conflagration of thunderous fire. In that moment the very elements of nature will be destroyed. That is, the universe itself will fall to pieces and be destroyed.

Here, then, is the reason behind the warning not to love the world or the things in the world. This is why 1 John 2:17 tells us that the world is passing away. That happens to be literally true. Our great God will one day dismantle this universe which has been so greatly stained by sin and marred through disobedience. He will start all over again. All that we regard as part of this life will disappear. Every mark of our current world system will be gone forever. Nothing will remain. Earth will not simply be renovated. It will be completely dismantled, destroyed, and totally re-created.

The New Jerusalem

Just as God had an earthly city called Jerusalem, so He will one day bring forth a heavenly city called the New Jerusalem. It will descend from heaven in the presence of

God to the new and re-created earth (Revelation 21:1–2). The scene will be dazzling as the saints of all ages watch the holy city, shimmering in all its splendor, slowly floating down through the clouds like a bride coming down the aisle to meet her beloved.

This passage answers a question believers have wondered about for centuries. We all know that we will spend eternity in heaven, but where will that be? The apostle John supplies the answer in his description of the New Jerusalem.

Face-to-Face

"Now the dwelling of God is with men, and he will live with them. They will be his people, and God himself will be with them and be their God" (21:3; see also 22:4). In these words are found the consummation of the dreams of all the ages. Immanuel! God with us. Not God far away in some distant place. Not God accessible only through the realm of prayer. But God *with* us, personally, intimately, face-to-face, with no distance, no barriers, but God and man together at last.

The Presence of Joy and the Absence of Pain

Verses 3–8 describe in some detail what will be included and excluded in the New Jerusalem. Interestingly, this passage tells us more about what won't be there than what will be there. John had no words to describe what he saw, so it was easier for him to tell what he didn't see. Here are some things that will be included in heaven: the personal presence of God (v. 3), eternal refreshment (v. 6), our eternal inheritance (v. 7), and intimate relationship with God (v. 7). What won't be in heaven? Tears (v. 4), death (v. 4), mourning (v. 4), pain (v. 4), and sinners (v. 8).

How can there be no more tears in heaven? Either we won't remember the things that brought us pain, or we will see them in a new light. Or perhaps they simply won't matter because we will be fully occupied with the praise and worship of God.

The sinners who are excluded from heaven include cowards, the unbelieving, vile people, murderers, the immoral, sorcerers, fortune-tellers and psychics, idolaters, and all liars. Not only will they not be there, but they wouldn't enjoy heaven if they were. No, the only place for such people is the lake of fire. Heaven wouldn't be heaven if vile people and murderers walked the streets. It would be too much like Chicago or New York or Miami or San Francisco.

The Glory of Heaven Is Jesus

The old chorus goes this way: "Heaven is a wonderful place, filled with glory and grace. I want to see my Savior's face. Heaven is a wonderful place." Heaven will truly be wonderful in every respect. It will be a place of eternal joy, eternal bliss, eternal rest, and eternal satisfaction. But the greatest wonder of heaven will be the personal presence of Jesus Christ.

The New Testament stresses this above everything else. Heaven is where Jesus is. When we are in heaven, we will see our loved ones again, but that will not be our greatest joy. We will meet the saints of all the ages, but that will be an extra benefit. In heaven we will drink the Water of Life and eat at the banquet table. We will walk the streets of gold and pick up precious jewels as if they were mere pebbles. But those things will be like a cherry perched atop a chocolate sundae. The glory of heaven will be Jesus. We will know Him and He will know us—all of us *by name*. Each one individually. And He won't need a name tag to recognize us.

All Things Made New

Verse 5 sums up heaven in this phrase: "I am making everything new!" New! What a wonderful word. We live in a world where things grow old and die, where our bodies wear down and run out, where new cars quickly become old heaps, where new homes eventually turn into dilapidated eyesores. Everything in this world soon rusts, falls apart, wears out, runs out, weakens, loosens, slows down, disintegrates, withers, decays, crumbles, and rots. No one lives forever, nothing lasts forever, all the buildings eventually fall down, every book turns to dust, and all the things made by the hand of man are like man himself—destined to return to the dust.

But heaven means new life, new hope, new bodies, new minds, new hearts, a new home, and a new start—the final and complete fulfillment of 2 Corinthians 5:17, "Old things are passed away; behold, all things are become new"! (KJV).

Heaven is thus a new place for new people who give up their old life for a new one supplied free of charge by the Lord Jesus Christ.

THE NEW JERUSALEM (REVELATION 21:9–22:6): VAST, DAZZLING, BEAUTIFUL

The angel invited John to inspect the New Jerusalem in greater detail (21:9–22:6). Again the city is described as the bride of Christ. It will be the eternal abode of the saints of God. This is the place Jesus has gone to prepare for His people (John 14:1–3).

It's outward appearance is brilliant, for it shines with the glory of God. In fact, the city appears to be crystal clear. Like Dorothy in the Wizard of Oz, who gasps as she sees the Emerald City in the distance, John is overwhelmed by the sight of the city. It is vast, dazzling, beautiful.

As John looks closer, he sees twelve gates in the massive walls surrounding the city. Each gate is manned by an angel, thus ensuring perfect security (Revelation 21:12). No one goes in or out without passing by the angelic guards. John also notices that the walls have twelve massive foundation stones (vv. 19–21).

The twelve gates represent the twelve tribes of Israel and the twelve foundation stones represent the twelve apostles. Thus, the city will be the abode of the saints of the Old Testament and the saints of the New Testament. All of the people of God from every age will live together in heaven for all eternity.

A Lawn So Big You'll Never Mow It by Yourself

John also adds fascinating details about the measurements of the city (vv. 15–17). It is fourteen hundred miles long, fourteen hundred miles wide, and fourteen hundred miles high! That's roughly the distance from the Pacific Ocean to the Mississippi River. It also means that the city is built either as a cube or pyramid that stretches far above the surface of the new earth. The walls are slightly over two hundred feet thick—roughly two-thirds the length of a football field.

If we assume that the city is a perfect cube, then the total amount of space would be 2,744,000,000 cubic miles. Let's also assume that 75 percent of that space is taken up with public buildings, parks, playgrounds, streets, forests, and other common areas. That leaves 686,000,000 cubic miles for private dwellings. If we further suppose that there will be 2 billion people in heaven, that gives every single man, woman, and child a little over one-third of a cubic mile of personal living space. You could easily build a fifty-thousand-square-foot mansion on that property and have plenty of space left over for a swimming pool, a tennis court, and a lawn so big that you would never be able to mow it by yourself.

Streets of Gold

Have you ever wondered why people talk about the streets of gold and the pearly gates? Perhaps you thought that was just folklore. Actually those word pictures come directly from this chapter. John specifies that the walls of the city are made of jasper (green quartz) and that the city itself is constructed of "pure gold, as pure as glass" (v. 18; see also v. 21). Evidently the foundations of the walls (vv. 19–20) are decorated with twelve kinds of precious stones: jasper (green), sapphire (blue), chalcedony (blue with stripes), emerald (green), sardonyx (red and white), carnelian (red), chrysolite (yellow gold), beryl (sea green), topaz (yellow), chrysoprase (apple green), jacinth (violet), and amethyst (purple).

Imagine twelve of the most precious stones Tiffany's could display laid on top of one another; not a few, not hundreds, not thousands, but millions of gemstones stretching as far as the eye can see, blending together in a fireworks display of splendor.

The twelve stones correspond roughly to the twelve precious stones on the breastplate of the high priest in the Old Testament. He was the only one who could go into the Holy of Holies, and that only once a year. But now the privileges of the High Priest are extended permanently to everyone in the New Jerusalem.

Eternal Light

John goes on to mention four things you won't find in heaven (21:22–25; see also 22:3–5). There will be *no temple,* for we will live forever in the personal presence of the Lord. There will be *no sun,* for the glory of God will be our light and the Lamb Himself will be our lamp. There will be *no moon,* for there will be *no night* in heaven.

What will we find in heaven? The Lord God Almighty, the Lamb, riches from every part of the earth, tribute from the rulers of the earth, the glory and honor of the nations, and a light that never goes out (vv. 22–26; see also 22:3–5).

As one who lives in a big city, that last part is most important to me personally. I happen to be writing these words late at night. Our doors are locked, and before I go to bed I will check them again. Like most major metropolitan areas, Chicago has many areas that aren't safe after dark. To be honest, I wouldn't dream of taking a walk outside right now. In the distance I can hear the sound of a siren. All of it reminds me that we live in a dangerous world where terrible things happen under cover of darkness.

It won't be that way in heaven because "there will be no night there" (v. 25; see also 22:5). Lest we misunderstand the implication, John goes on to say that no impure person or deceitful person or shameful person will ever enter the city of God, but only those whose names are written in the Lamb's Book of Life (v. 27).

Literal or Figurative?

Of all the questions we might ask about Revelation 21, the chief one is this: Is this literal or is it figurative? Are the streets of heaven truly paved with gold and are the gates actually made of pearl, or are those things symbols of something else?

The answer of course is yes. Yes, these things are literal, and yes, they are symbolic. What John saw was a city of gold with streets of gold. But the gold he saw was completely transparent, so it wasn't earthly gold at all. He saw a huge gate made of one pearl. So obviously it is not a pearl as we know pearls.

Heaven will be nothing like what I have described in this chapter. My words are too small, my imagination too puny, my vision too limited by my earthly experience. Heaven is more than streets of gold and gates of pearl, but it is not less than that.

MORE WONDERFUL THAN WE CAN IMAGINE

In one of his sermons, the late Senate chaplain Peter Marshall gave an illustration that went something like this:

Before a baby is born, it can recognize its mother's voice. If you shine a light into the womb, the baby will react to it. If you push the baby, it will kick your hand away. How much does that unborn child understand of life outside the womb? Not much, just the sound of one or two voices and the sensation of movement. Inside the womb the baby feels safe and secure.

If you could somehow converse with the child, he would be very confident in discoursing about what life will be like once he is born. His discussion would rest on what he has already experienced. In the womb he swims, moves, tosses and turns, quiets to the sound of his mother's voice, and reacts to her emotions and to sudden movements, and he expects more of the same once he is born.

What a shock awaits him when he suddenly slides through the birth canal (a harrowing, terrifying experience) only to find himself being held upside down in the glare of bright lights and loud voices. *Who are these people? Why are they wearing masks? Why am I so cold? And why is this person slapping my bottom? I didn't do anything wrong. Where is my mother?*

For a few seconds, the baby feels totally abandoned. Then he hears a voice—a tender, melodious voice he has come to know, clearer now than he's ever heard it before, "Come here, sweetheart." Someone takes him toward the voice and he settles in, listening to that one voice he knows, resting above her heart. He has no idea where he is or what has happened. He does not know what will happen next. But when the baby hears his mother's voice, he knows that all will be well.

The Sound of Laughter

In this life we are like that unborn child. We know as much of life after death as the unborn child knows of life after birth. We hear the sound of laughter coming from the other side and stories of a great city unlike any we have ever known. It seems so fantastic as to be almost magic. Like that unborn child, we comfort ourselves that we know much about heaven, but in reality we know so little that we hardly know anything at all.

In the days to come we will all pass through the valley of the shadow of death. Most of us will find this experience harrowing and perhaps terrifying. We will feel as if we have been abandoned by those we leave behind. We will wonder if anyone will be there to meet us on the other side, or even if there *is* another side. Everything will be dark and frightening. All that we have believed will seem to be for naught.

But on the other side of death we will be as surprised as that newborn baby. The sounds! The lights! The voices! The angels! The singing! The vast throngs of people! The endless rush of the river of life! We will rub our eyes to see if we are dreaming. For a few moments nothing will make sense. *Where am I? If I'm not dreaming, what kind of place is this? Why is everything so bright, why are those children playing so happily? Where did I come from and how did I get here?*

Where All Your Dreams Come True

You are in heaven, where all your best dreams finally come true. Nothing is what you expected. It's better, brighter, more beautiful. Nothing you ever imagined was anything like heaven. Suddenly you look down and say to yourself, "That must be the street of gold." It's not at all like you thought it would be, but when you see it, you realize it couldn't be anything else.

Then your mind begins to focus. Ah, your mind, sharper now, all those cobwebs gone; you can think faster than ever, you're so smart now that Einstein is like a dunce compared to you. And your body—you never looked so good. Your feet—you can run for miles and not grow weary. Your arms—so strong. Your face, your hair, your eyes—they're all yours, but you've never seen them before. It's you, no question about that, but it's not like any *you* you've ever seen.

Amazingly, you seem to know lots of people in this new place. In fact, it's as if you've known them all forever. Suddenly you've got 2 billion of the nicest next-door neighbors anyone ever had.

Dinner with the King

Shhh! What was that? Did you hear trumpets blow? Yes. It's almost noon and the King of New Jerusalem has invited the entire kingdom to a feast. Does He do this often, you ask? Every day, they say. So you follow the crowds to the vast plaza, find your place near the head table, standing while the King arrives. You recognize Him from a distance. He looks like a lion and a lamb and a man! It's Jesus. You would have known Him anywhere. When He begins to speak, tears well up within you. His voice! It's unlike any you've ever heard, but it's the same voice you heard in your other life on earth. But louder, clearer, the most beautiful sound in the universe.

This is heaven. All you've hoped for, all you've waited for, far more than you dreamed of. You are in heaven. It's nothing like you imagined but just what you wanted. You're home now, home in heaven, home where you belong. At home in heaven, the eternal abode of the people of God.

What I have written is fictional but true. Heaven will be like that, only much better. Is Revelation 21–22 literal? Absolutely, but believe me, it's nothing like we've imagined. Get ready to be surprised. You're going to be laughing for the first ten thousand years.

14

A VERY PERSONAL STATEMENT OF FAITH

Tonight I sit and stare at the blank face of my computer. It's dark outside, and the boys are in bed. In the kitchen the dishwasher drones, and in the bedroom I hear Marlene talking to someone on the phone—I can't quite tell who it is. Somewhere in the distance a dog barks at a passing car. Things are peaceful in my corner of the world.

Yesterday I had barely gotten to work when Marlene called and said that Buddy McCallum was dying. It wasn't really a surprise; he's had cancer for quite a while, surgery two years ago, and then surgery again last November. I hadn't seen him since then, until two or three weeks ago when we—Marlene and I—dropped by his house. The cancer had done its grim work. He was thin, down to 119 pounds, he said, from 166 pounds before the last operation. He was weak but he looked good, and I could tell he was glad to see us. We sat down and talked about his upcoming treatment—something called Interferon, a wonder drug that might or might not make a difference. But Buddy was hopeful, and so we talked about it. After a few minutes, we prayed together and then Marlene and I got up to leave. Buddy walked with us to the door. He gripped my hand, Marlene hugged him, and he said over and over how glad he was that we came by.

That was a couple of weeks ago. Then another call came yesterday. My dear friend is dying of cancer. The Interferon didn't work. Buddy has stopped eating or drinking, his weight is down to 110, and the doctors have told him there is no hope. In a day or two they will send him home to die.

One of the family members called and said that when he dies they want me to do the funeral. I buried his wife, Lois, two years ago. His only son died at the age of ten. And Buddy may die this week.

This week. Easter week. Holy week. What a week for someone to die. I sit tonight and ponder what it is I really believe. I may well have a funeral to do before I attend the Easter Sunrise Service this Sunday morning.

I BELIEVE IN GOD

Death has a way of concentrating the mind. In a blinding flash of reality, we see that many of the things we thought were important really aren't. And some of the great truths we took for granted turn out in the moment of crisis to be the rocks on which we steady our shaking souls.

So I say quite simply that I believe in God. For me there is no doubt on that point. Behind our questions, our doubts, our fears, our nagging worries, our sleepless nights—behind it all, there is God who created the heavens and the earth. We neither see Him nor hear Him nor touch Him. And though we search to the ends of the earth, we will not find Him. Not even in our books of theology. But He is there, nonetheless, and if we seek Him with all our hearts, we will find Him. The theologians call it paradox and mystery and antinomy, but it doesn't really matter what you call it. He is there. He has always been there. He will always be there. When the last monument to the creative genius of mankind has crumbled into the dust, He will still be there—eternal, enthroned, the sovereign of the universe.

And I believe that God has spoken to us in the Bible. That seems wonderfully clear to me tonight. The God who cannot be seen or heard or touched—the God who rules over all creation—that God has spoken to us. What He has said is true. As the confession says, it is truth without any admixture of error. There is no error in it because there is no error in God. What He says is true and reliable and trustworthy, not just the message but every little detail as well. Therefore, when the Bible says, "In my Father's house are many rooms" (John 14:2), I believe it to be true, though I really do not know what it means. But I rest my soul on this: If God has said it, then it must be true. I smile as I reflect on the fact that Buddy will understand those words in a few days. In moments like these, the fact that I believe the Bible is God's Word makes all the difference in the world.

And I believe that God loves us. Loves me. Loves all the Buddy McCallums of the world. Loves every man, no matter how wretched. And I really do believe that God has a wonderful plan for every man and every woman. I believe it, for why else would God send His Son to die on the cross? I wouldn't do it. I wouldn't send one of my sons to die. But God did. Love starts with God, and it comes rolling down to us by way of the bloody cross. The wonder of God's love is this: It starts with Him and not with us.

WIPED CLEAN AND BORN AGAIN

Two years ago when I preached Lois's funeral I used her Bible and found some notes she had written in the margin next to Romans 5:1. I don't remember what she wrote or what I said, but I remember the text. "Therefore being justified by faith, we have peace with God through our Lord Jesus Christ" (KJV). Justification: that act of God whereby guilty sinners are declared righteous on the basis of the death of Jesus Christ. Not *made* righteous, at least not in this life. But *declared* righteous, judicially acquitted, forgiven, the slate wiped clean, and the righteousness of Jesus Christ credited to us. The one thing we spend our lives striving for, acceptance, we never find because we keep falling short; but in one moment of faith, God gives it to us. And it all comes through our Lord Jesus Christ. *Lord:* His deity; *Jesus:* the Savior; *Christ:* God's Anointed Deliverer. The end of it all is that we have peace with God in life and in death.

I believe that sinful men and women can be born again by putting their faith in Jesus Christ. That is, they can literally be born again. They can be converted, changed, radically transformed. In a world where vast promises are made for everything new, from new cars to soda pop, here is one promise that is both vast and true: "If anyone is in Christ, he is a new creation" (2 Corinthians 5:17). The new birth is more than a religious slogan; it is a reality for those who put their faith in Jesus Christ.

Salvation, then, is a free gift of God. It is received on the single condition of trusting in Jesus Christ, whose death on the cross is the full payment for man's sin. Those who are thus born again can never be unborn. They have a security that is eternal; and, therefore, in the words of my friend Jack Wyrtzen, they are as sure of heaven as if they had already been there ten thousand years.

I believe that the new life which Jesus Christ provides is made possible through the indwelling ministry of the Holy Spirit. Furthermore, I believe that without the Holy Spirit there is no way to live the Christian life. There is no combination of human effort and good intentions that can enable us to do what God has asked us to do. The old Youth for Christ doctrinal statement puts it with beautiful simplicity: "We believe in the present ministry of the Holy Spirit by whose indwelling the Christian is able to live a godly life."

This simply means that when I need Him—which is all the time—He is always there.

FROM HERE TO MOMBASSA

During this Holy Week I believe in the church universal—the great body of believers scattered from Mombassa to Lisbon to Minsk to Darwin to Asuncion to Juneau. In more churches than I can imagine, believers are recounting the final days of our Lord. And this Sunday in a thousand tongues they will sing of His resurrection. They are my brothers and my sisters. They are part of God's great worldwide family. And between them and me, though we are separated by thousands of miles and vast cultural differences, there is true spiritual unity.

If you want to know the truth, I still believe in the local church. More than ever, I still believe. After nearly twenty years as a pastor, seeing all that is good and some that is not so good, I still believe that the local church is the centerpiece of God's plan in the world today. Nothing will ever take its place.

We come to church on Sunday with our minds racing in a thousand directions. It's been a hard week, filled with long days and busy nights. Then Sunday comes at last. When we come to church our friends are there, they greet us at the door, we laugh and talk, we sit together, we sing the hymns and pray the prayers. The pastor preaches. We stand for the benediction and out we go. But we are not the same. Something has happened. We have met God there. It's another one of those mysteries, but God is there on Sunday when the family comes together.

I know that in the church things sometimes move slowly and progress is hard to see. But it doesn't matter, for God has chosen the church as His primary means of blessing the world. We needn't be ashamed or feel as though we have to apologize for our imperfections. God is there in the midst of His people, and His plan is being worked out in the church and, in ways we can hardly understand, He is being glorified.

"Son, You're Looking in the Wrong Place"

Finally, I believe in the return of Jesus Christ to the earth—the personal, visible, bodily, imminent return of our Lord. And I believe in the resurrection of the dead. A pastor friend told me a few years ago that he believes every church should recite the Apostles' Creed every Sunday because it contains the phrase, "I believe in the resurrection of the body." That doctrine is so hard for modern man to believe that we need to repeat it every Sunday to remind ourselves it is true.

I am faced with an awful dilemma tonight. My friend Buddy McCallum is dying, and I can't do anything about it. But it's Holy Week, and before long Easter will be here. How do these two so different things fit together?

Many years ago I was asked to perform a graveside service for a man I barely knew. I was young and inexperienced and thought to say a few words of comfort. I fumbled my way through the ceremony and came to the closing prayer. When I got to the part about the resurrection of the dead, the words stuck in my throat. I could barely finish my prayer. I went back home frustrated and embarrassed. What had gone wrong? Then it hit me. I wasn't sure I believed in the resurrection of the dead. Up until then, it had all been theoretical. But now I had come face-to-face with death, and all my brave words seemed so hollow.

Out of that experience I began to pray, and it seemed as if God said to me, "Son, you're looking in the wrong place. There is indeed a grave that's empty, but it's over on the other side of the world, outside Jerusalem, carved into a mountainside. That tomb is empty, and it's been empty for two thousand years."

Several years ago I visited the Holy Land for the first time. During our visit to Jerusalem, we spent an hour at the

210

Garden Tomb, the spot believed by many to be the actual burial place of Jesus. It is located about two hundred yards from Gordon's Calvary, that strange rock outcropping that appears to be worn into the shape of a skull. We know it was used as a burial site in Jesus' day. Many believe it was the spot of the Crucifixion.

The Garden Tomb is located in a beautiful garden built over an ancient Roman aqueduct. To your left as you enter the garden is a typical first-century tomb dug into the hillside. A trench in front of the opening was apparently designed for the massive stone that once covered the entrance.

NO BODY THERE

Because the opening is very small, I had to duck to go inside. For a few seconds, you see nothing until your eyes adjust to the darkness. Then you can easily make out the two chambers. Visitors stand in the mourners' chamber. A wrought-iron fence protects the chamber where the body was laid. You soon notice that the burial chamber was originally designed for two bodies. However, one ledge was never finished for some reason. The other one was. It appears to be designed for a person slightly less than six feet tall.

As I looked around the burial chamber, I could see faint markings left by Christian pilgrims from earlier centuries. After a few seconds another thought enters the mind. *There is no body to be found in this tomb. Whoever was buried here evidently left a long time ago. The Garden Tomb is empty!*

As you exit into the sunlight, your eyes fasten upon a wooden sign: "Why seek ye the living among the dead? He is not here, for He is risen, as He said."

"LOOK WHAT I DID FOR MY SON"

We look at our loved ones dying and wonder if the resurrection can be true. But that's backwards. God says, "Look what I did for my Son. Will I do any less for those who put their trust in Him? Put simply: We do not believe in the resurrection of the dead because of anything we can see with our eyes; everything we see argues against it. People die all the time. There hasn't been a resurrection in a long, long time. No, we believe in the resurrection of the saints because we believe in the resurrection of Jesus. "We believe that Jesus died and rose again and so we believe that God will bring with Jesus those who have fallen asleep in him" (1 Thessalonians 4:14).

And so tonight I have no doubts about my friend Buddy. He may not make it through the week, but he's going to be all right. God has promised to take care of him, and He will. And if I preach a funeral this week, I'll do it in full confidence that the funeral is not the end of the story.

That's what the return of Christ means to me. The suffering we see around us—the wasting disease, the incredible pain of broken lives—thank God that is not the end of the story. There are better days ahead: The Rapture, the victorious return, Christ reigning as King in the very place where He was crucified. And best of all, as the apostle Paul put it, "We will be with the Lord forever" (1 Thessalonians 4:17).

FIVE DAYS FROM EASTER

It's late now, and the house is very quiet. On this day Jesus cursed the fig tree. Tomorrow He faced down the Pharisees. The next day He met with His disciples in the Upper Room. On the next day He was crucified. The day after that He lay in the tomb. And on Sunday—just five days from now—He rose from the dead.

Someone said, "Wouldn't it be sad if Buddy died this week?" I don't think so. No, it wouldn't be sad at all. I can't think of a better time to die than during the week before Jesus rose from the dead. After all, everything we really believe comes down to what happened that week. If it's true, then we're in great shape. And the good news—the gospel truth, as they say down South—is that it's true, it really happened. And that means that whether we live or die, we're in great shape tonight.

15

OUR RESPONSIBILITY

I have conducted more heartbreaking funerals in the last six months than I have during any other period in the nineteen years I have been a pastor. In one week I buried two forty-two-year-old men who had died of cancer. Later I spoke a funeral service for a premature baby who was born three months early and died after two days. As I left that room in the funeral home, I went across the hall to comfort a wife whose husband had dropped dead while he was walking into the hospital.

As the years pass, it doesn't get any easier. And the questions remain. Just today I received a message from one of our missionaries. A beloved colleague was terribly injured in an automobile accident. Although he lived for a week, he died suddenly in the middle of the night. With total honesty the missionary bared his soul.

> My heart is in shock. Why, God? Noel and his wife Jill gave up their current professions to serve God as youth pastor missionaries. Noel is especially built for being a youth pastor. God designed Noel with such passion in life. And more than that, passion toward people. And more than that, passion toward God. He has constantly been a source of encouragement. Why, God? I really don't understand. I really don't

even pretend to understand. I have so many questions. God, why Noel? And why now? After such an encouraging comeback for a whole week! God is so weird. I am not saying bad, but weird. I do not understand Him.

Why? Why now? Why this? How could God do such a thing?

It is easier to ask the questions than to answer them. And any answer will seem pitifully inadequate, especially to the one suffering such a loss. But the missionary is also a Christian, and he provided part of his own answer. It was raining hard when he heard the news of his colleague's death. The thought occurred to him that it only takes a few degrees difference in temperature to change rain into snow. Rain, he said, speaks of death, depression, and sorrow, while snow speaks of freshness, life, and heaven. Then he drew this conclusion:

> Just a few degrees change. In water the change is so very small. The change from the earthly plane to the spiritual seems so very great . . . at least from the earthly viewpoint. Noel being in Heaven seems so crystal clear. Clear to what I do not know, but it seems so good. I still have a whole lot of Why? questions for God. And at times I ask them out of anger. But at the same time, they don't seem as significant in light of seeing a vivid picture of Noel enjoying Heaven and God our Father delighting in Noel.

In every great moment of crisis, we all have a choice to make. Either we will choose to believe in God or we won't. More specifically, we will choose to believe that God is good or we won't. In the times of pain and loss, that choice must be made by faith, not because of what has happened, but often in spite of it.

I cannot prove to you that God is good any more than I can prove the existence of heaven or that Jesus Christ is the Son of God. I can simply tell you what the Bible says and what the people of God have discovered across the centuries.

Choosing to believe that God is good will not exempt you from sorrow and suffering, nor will it guarantee you an easy road to follow. But it will put a firm foundation beneath your feet as you journey from earth to heaven. As I close this book, I am drawn again to the words of A. J. Gossip, who said to those who wondered why he still believed in God after his wife's tragic death, "You people in the sunshine may believe the faith, but we in the shadow must believe it. We have nothing else."

I've thought a lot about that in the last few months. Death comes to all of us sooner or later, and we will all spend time in the school of suffering. Sometimes the road does indeed become very steep and the way very dark. But we have a wonderful God.

If you believe that, you can face things that would destroy most people. Indeed, if you believe that, you can face your own death with confidence and courage.

One final word from Pastor Gossip. "I don't think you need to be afraid of life." There is a reason the Bible calls Him the God of all comfort. It is in His very nature to comfort His people in all their afflictions. With that confidence we can go forward one step at a time, walking into the future without fear, taking all that life has to offer—the good and the bad together, even when some questions remain unanswered.

He is the God of all comfort. Fear not, and keep on believing in Him.

Moody Press, a ministry of Moody Bible Institute,
is designed for education, evangelization, and edification.
If we may assist you in knowing more about Christ
and the Christian life, please write us without obligation:
Moody Press, c/o MLM, Chicago, Illinois 60610.